T H E
UNOFFICIAL
U.S.
CENSUS

Also by Tom Heymann

ON AN AVERAGE DAY . . .

ON AN AVERAGE DAY IN THE SOVIET UNION . . .

T H E
UNOFFICIAL
U.S.
CENSUS

Tom Heymann

FAWCETT COLUMBINE

NEW YORK

DEDICATION

To my daughter,
and newest love,
Laura.

A Fawcett Columbine Book
Published by Ballantine Books
Copyright © 1991 by Thomas N. Heymann

Library of Congress Catalog Card Number: 91-70449
ISBN: 0-449-90622-1

Cover design by Dale Fiorillo
Text design by Beth Tondreau Design/Mary A. Wirth

Manufactured in the United States of America
First Edition: May 1991
10 9 8 7 6 5 4 3 2 1

Acknowledgments

I want to thank my friend, and research assistant, Alec Rabinowitz, for his hard work and sense of humor. Also, thanks to my friends, and literary agents, Herbert and Nancy Katz, for their insistence that it be done "right." Also to my editor, Elisa Wares, for her hard work and enthusiasm. Finally, to my wife, Grace, and my son, Gabriel, for letting me work.

Introduction

Every ten years, the federal government assembles a team of 520,000 census-takers to compile an exact statistical portrait of the United States.

Using the latest research methods and computer technology, the U.S. government spends more than $2.6 billion creating its study. As part of its effort, the government delivers a questionnaire to every American home. Nearly one million of these homes are also visited by a Census Department employee.

Working from his home-based office, Tom Heymann spends untold hundreds of dollars compiling data for his unofficial census. Information is drawn from a variety of credible mainstream and alternative sources including: private and public research agencies; public interest groups; trade associations; product marketers; news services; scientific journals; newspapers; and a host of other organizations and experts.

At the completion of its study, the U.S. government publishes *The Official Census of the United States*. The government's report analyzes population growth, migration, education, home ownership, marriages, births, deaths, and a range of other serious subjects.

At the completion of his study, Heymann publishes *The Unofficial U.S. Census*. Included in his report are many subject areas left unexamined by the U.S. government and vitally important to any comprehensive study of the American way of life.

While the government's census features many of our more mundane subject areas, the *Unofficial Census* focuses on the sometimes seamy, often embarrassing, and always revealing underside of American life.

For example, while the government's report lists the number of psychiatrists who live in the United States, the *Unofficial Census* reveals how many of these Americans are involved in sexual relationships with their clients. And while the government's census includes the number of dogs and cats who live in America, the *Unofficial Census* divulges the number who sleep in their owner's bed.

Whether it concerns population size, gender, age, or any other demographic aspect of American life, the *Unofficial Census* approaches each subject area from a new and distinct angle.

And while the United States census tells Americans what the government feels they need to know, the *Unofficial Census* tells Americans what they will enjoy knowing.

T H E
UNOFFICIAL
U.S.
CENSUS

Number Born
Unintentionally

Of the nearly 250 million Americans alive today, more than one-third, 86,205,000 were the result of unwanted pregnancies.

Of these Americans who were "born anyway," 60,343,500 were the result of mistimed pregnancies.

The remaining 25,861,500 were the result of unwanted births.

NOTE: It should be remembered that children who were the result of mistimed or unwanted births do not necessarily become "unwanted" children and adults.

Number Born by Artificial Means

A great deal of attention has been focused recently on the growing use of artificial methods of conception. A surprisingly large number of Americans alive today were conceived with the help of modern science.

Included in this category are 6,800 Americans who began their lives as "test tube babies."

Also included are an additional 4,000 Americans who were born from artificially inseminated surrogate mothers.

NOTE: 65,000 Americans are conceived each year by artificial insemination. Of these births, 35,000 utilize the husband's sperm, while the remaining 30,000 are the product of a donor's sperm.

Distribution by Month Born

The Unofficial Census counted Americans by the month in which they were born:

Month	Number Born
January	21,181,800
February	20,369,010
March	22,167,000
April	20,024,190
May	21,354,210
June	20,031,579
July	20,361,621
August	21,181,800
September	22,832,010
October	17,413,410
November	19,038,990
December	20,361,621

Distribution by Astrological Sign

Despite the fact that only 1 in 4 Americans will admit to believing in astrology, every American knows his or her astrological sign. The Unofficial Census counted Americans by their involuntary membership in these heavenly bodies:

Astrological Sign	Number Born Under That Sign
Aries (March 20–April 20)	19,383,810
Taurus (April 20–May 21)	21,994,590
Gemini (May 21–June 21)	21,181,800
Cancer (June 21–July 22)	20,196,600
Leo (July 22–August 23)	20,861,610
Virgo (August 23–September 23)	21,674,400
Libra (September 23–October 23)	20,689,200
Scorpio (October 23–November 22)	17,241,000
Sagittarius (November 22–December 21)	18,891,210
Capricorn (December 21–January 20)	18,883,821
Aquarius (January 20–February 19)	21,354,210
Pisces (February 19–March 20)	23,964,990

Counting Parapsychologists

Parapsychologists study phenomena that can not be explained by any known laws of nature. Areas of parapsychology research include telepathy, clairvoyance, and psychokinesis (the moving of objects by psychic power). We turned our sights toward this elusive subject:

✎ There are 200 Americans working as professional parapsychologists.

✎ Of these individuals, 98 work for private corporations and 2 are employed by the federal government.

✎ The country's remaining 100 parapsychologists work as private crime investigators.

Psychics—Distribution by Services Rendered and Earnings

A surprisingly large number of Americans are working as psychics. Of these individuals, 50,000 are working at their craft full-time, while the remaining half are part-timers.

Of these professionals, 25,000 report earnings of more than $25,000 from their practices, while at least 300 earn in excess of $50,000.

Our nation's psychics offer the following professional services: 5,000 read crystal balls, 5,000 conduct seances, and 3,000 read palms.

Additionally, 20,000 psychics include "communicating with the dead" as one of the services they provide.

# THE UNOFFICIAL U.S. CENSUS

Believers in Miracles

A large majority of American adults, 125,856,000 persons, believe in miracles.

Of these believers, 70,044,683 are women, and 55,184,395 are men.

Visions—Number Experiencing

Visions are feelings that you have seen faraway events as they are happening. The Unofficial Census counted the number of Americans who claim to have experienced visions.

As we learned, nearly 1 in 4 American adults, 42 million persons, claim to have had visions.

Of these "super sighted" Americans, 16 million have had visions more than once or twice, and 4 million have the experience frequently.

THE
UNOFFICIAL
U.S.
CENSUS

ESP—Number Experiencing

The Unofficial Census counted the number of Americans who claim to have experienced ESP.

As we discovered, more than half of American adults, 102 million persons, claim to have had ESP.

Of these "extrasensory Americans," 51 million have had ESP more than once or twice and 12 million have ESP frequently.

Déjà Vu—Number Experiencing

Déjà vu is the illusion that you have already experienced something that you are actually experiencing for the first time. The Unofficial Census counted the number of Americans who claim to have experienced déjà vu.

As we discovered, nearly two-thirds of American adults, 116 million persons, claim to have had a déjà vu experience.

Of these Americans, 62 million claim to have had the experience more than once or twice, and 12 million have déjà vu experiences frequently.

Hypnotists—
Distribution by Type
of Professional Activity

There are 25,000 hypnotists working in America.

Of these, only a small number, 1,250, are working as stage performers.

Of the country's remaining 23,750 hypnotists, most perform hypnotherapy for behavior modification objectives (weight loss, smoking cessation, etc.).

NOTE: The percentage of hypnotists practicing their craft for entertainment purposes has decreased radically in the last thirty years. Perhaps as a result of the growth in the field of behavior modification, the percentage of hypnotists working as performers has shrunk from 95 percent in 1951 to just 5 percent today.

THE
UNOFFICIAL
U.S.
CENSUS

Counting Ghosts and Their "Busters"

An astounding 25 percent of American adults, 45,600,000 persons, believe in ghosts. This number represents an increase of more than 100 percent since 1978. The Unofficial Census couldn't help but investigate this phenomenon further.

As we learned, there are an estimated 100 professional ghost investigators—"ghost busters"—working in America.

Of these individuals, 3 make a very comfortable living from their craft, earning more than $100,000 annually. Another 47, however, are struggling to make ends meet, earning less than $10,000 each year.

NOTE: Who said that opposites attract? 4 out of 5 ghost investigators are married to others in the same profession.

Satanists—Dimension and Nature of Practice

The Unofficial Census looked at the number of Satanists (Devil-worshipers) who reside in America.

As we discovered, there are approximately 15,000 Americans who are currently involved in Satanism.

Of these, a large number offer living sacrifices, including 1,500 who sacrifice animals (cats, dogs, etc.) and 150 who prefer to use human beings.

Witches and Warlocks— Distribution by Sex, Religion, etc.

The Unofficial Census turned its attention to the subject of witchcraft in America. We dug up some interesting facts regarding our nation's sorcerers and sorceresses.

As we discovered, there are approximately 15,000 Americans who practice witchcraft.

Of these, 4,500 are warlocks (male witches).

Many witches can be characterized by their prior departure from mainstream religions. Included in this category are 12,000 former Catholics, and 750 former Jews.

Additionally, it is reported that 1,500 witches are gay or bisexual, while an equal number are under the age of 13.

Vampires, by Method of Blood Acquisition

Vampires, it turns out, are more than just the featured fictional characters of late-night horror films. There are an estimated 500 vampires walking the streets of America. The Unofficial Census decided to take a closer look at the methods behind the madness of this strange obsession.

It turns out that a majority of this nation's vampires, 425, prefer to use the "biting method" when they go in search of their life-sustaining beverage.

Our remaining 75 vampires prefer to use syringes and other cutting instruments to acquire their blood supply.

Blood Donors and Recipients

Americans are constantly being prodded to donate blood. But how many actually do so and how many of us require these donations? The Unofficial Census looked into this bloody issue.

As our research indicates, 14,778,000 Americans donate blood.

Our findings also reveal that a smaller number of Americans, 4,926,000, receive blood transfusions each year. Many of these recipients require several transfusions consecutively.

NOTE: Due to a chronic shortage in the United States, blood is now being imported from foreign countries. Of the 12 million units of blood transfused in the U.S. each year, more than 28,000 units are imported from Europe. While 40 percent of the U.S. population is eligible to donate blood (the others are screened out because of age or health), only 6 percent of Americans donate.

**U.S. Blood
Type Clusters**

With growing uncertainty about the safety of the nation's blood supply, Americans are becoming more aware of their blood types. Some Americans are even going so far as to maintain a private supply of their own frozen blood in the event they need a transfusion.

The Unofficial Census counted the number of Americans having certain blood types:

BLOOD TYPE	NUMBER HAVING
O +	91,131,000
A +	88,668,000
B +	22,167,000
O –	17,241,000
A –	14,778,000
AB +	7,389,000
B –	4,926,000
AB –	2,463,000

NOTE: Type O blood is the most common and is called the "universal donor" because it can be given to people with any blood type.

THE
UNOFFICIAL
U.S.
CENSUS

Looking at Skinny-dippers

More than 1 in 10 American adults, 23 million persons, have gone "skinny dipping."

These exhibitionists may be found, and observed, at any of America's 200 nude beaches.

Not surprisingly, 50 of the nation's nude beaches are located in California.

Naturists, by Type of Sunscreen Used

Naturists believe that clothes should be optional equipment.

Of the 17,500 free-thinking Americans who are members of the Naturist Society, 875 do not use any sunscreen when they sunbathe.

Of those who prefer some protection from the sun, the largest number, 3,850, use Coppertone products. Another 2,275 use Johnson & Johnson products, while 2,100 prefer Hawaiian Tropic.

Tanning Injuries, by Source and Number Reported

With the recent dramatic rise in skin cancer rates, the value of a golden tan has lost some of its luster. A number of Americans, however, continue to accept the risks as they search for the perfect tan. The Unofficial Census turned its sights toward this burning issue.

As we discovered, more than 2 million Americans use commercial tanning facilities.

At least 3,300 indoor tanners will be taken to emergency rooms this year for burn injuries related to their use of suntan booths and sunlamps.

Of these emergency room patrons, 700 will be burned in suntanning booths and 2,600 will be burned while using sunlamps.

NOTE: There are approximately 10,000 commercial tanning facilities in the U.S. Despite the fact that 96 percent of Americans know that exposure to the sun can be dangerous, 66 percent of Americans still think that tans ''look healthy'' and 33 percent of Americans still work to get tan. On a more positive note, however, more Americans are using sunscreens, and more are getting less sun because of their increased fears of the sun's harmful effects.

Musical Americans and Their Choice of Instruments

Music is an important part of the lives of many Americans. In an effort to learn which instruments Americans are most likely to play, the Unofficial Census set out in search of some answers.

Our findings indicate that more than 57,000,000 Americans play a musical instrument. Of those, nearly half play more than one instrument and a majority (78%) play regularly.

Americans play the following instruments in greatest number:

Musical Instrument	Number Playing
Piano	20,600,000
Guitar	18,900,000
Organ	6,300,000
Flute	4,000,000
Clarinet	4,000,000
Drums	3,000,000
Trumpet	2,900,000
Violin	2,300,000
Harmonica	1,700,000
Saxophone	1,100,000
Electronic keyboards	600,000

Counting Those With Perfect Pitch

While a majority of Americans enjoy music, and millions play a musical instrument, only a relatively small number have perfect pitch—the ability to recognize an isolated note or to sing a note without first hearing it.

An estimated 164,000 Americans are the heirs to perfect pitch.

NOTE: It is widely believed that perfect pitch runs in families. It is also believed that the presence of perfect pitch does not increase the likelihood that a person will become a talented musician.

Musicians Injured Playing Their Instruments

Our research reveals that musicians are particularly susceptible to injury.

For example, of the 20,600,000 Americans who play the piano, a majority have sustained injuries as a result of their playing.

14,214,000 American pianists have sustained back injuries, while 7,828,000 American pianists have sustained neck injuries.

NOTE: While pianists are most likely to suffer neck injuries, cellists and harpists are more likely to incur back disorders. As many as 75 percent of professional musicians have suffered serious injuries from playing their instruments.

THE
UNOFFICIAL
U.S.
CENSUS

Stamps, by Number Collecting

A large group of Americans view stamps as something more than the way to pay for a letter's postage. The Unofficial Census counted our nation's philatelists (stamp collectors).

As of the latest count, there are more than 2 million stamp collectors in America.

A large majority of these, 1.8 million, are men.

Coins, by Number Collecting

Coins are legal tender and, as such, help us pay for goods and services. For a large number of Americans, however, they also make favorite collectibles. The Unofficial Census counted our nation's numismatists (coin collectors).

As of the latest count, there are more than 3 million coin collectors in America.

As with their philatelic relatives, a large majority of numismatists, 2,850,000, are men.

What's more, nearly 2 million of these collectors started their hobby as kids.

Strange Hobbies—Distribution by Number Pursuing

Most Americans know somebody who collects stamps, coins, or bottle caps. But what are some of the country's more unusual hobbies? The Unofficial Census counted some of our country's stranger special interest groups.

As we discovered, Americans are involved in a number of esoteric pursuits:

HOBBY OR CLUB	NUMBER INVOLVED
The Official Star Trek Fan Club	50,000
The Andy Griffith Rerun Watchers Club	15,000
The Royal Association for Longevity and Preservation of the Honeymooners	12,000
Fast Draw Competitions	350
Ship in bottle collecting	300
Police car collecting	200

Candy Making and Other Pursuits— Number Participating

Great numbers of Americans are involved in a variety of crafts and hobbies. The Unofficial Census counted Americans by their participation in certain activities:

CRAFT OR HOBBY	NUMBER INVOLVED
Sewing/needlecrafts	46,415,000
Candy making/cake decorating	14,852,800
Painting/drawing	13,924,500
Plastic model kits	11,139,600
Ceramics	9,283,000
Flowers/silk making	8,354,700
Macrame	7,426,400
Doll Collecting	6,498,100
Model railroading	5,569,800

Doodlers

Americans are engaged in some common activities that may appear strange when exposed to the light of day. Take doodling as one example. As we might expect, a majority of American adults, more than 136,800,000 persons, doodle.

As the following table illustrates, these Americans are motivated to doodle by a variety of circumstances:

Motivation for Doodling	Number
Talking on telephone	86,184,000
Boredom	82,080,000
Thinking/problem-solving	75,240,000
To relax	57,456,000

NOTE: America's doodlers tend to be female, young, and wealthy.

Counting Horseshoe Pitchers

President Bush's passion for horseshoe pitching has focused a great deal of attention on this relatively quiet sport. The Unofficial Census decided that a closer look was essential.

Approximately 9.9 million Americans pitch horseshoes.

Of these pitchers, a large majority, 8.3 million, are men.

Also forming a majority, 6 million pitchers, are those over 50 years of age. Only a minority of today's pitchers, 1.2 million, are younger than 30 years old.

NOTE: President Bush, it seems, has had a favorable impact on the sport. Membership in the National Horseshoe Pitchers Association has grown to 17,000, from just 4,000 in 1985. Sales of horseshoe equipment have grown similarly.

THE
UNOFFICIAL
U.S.
CENSUS

Bowling Ball and Bowling Shoe Owners

Bowling is one of America's favorite pastimes. But how many bowlers take the sport seriously? The Unofficial Census took a closer look at America's bowlers and their purchases of bowling equipment.

According to our research findings, the following trends in bowling ball, and bowling shoe, ownership have emerged:

✎ More than 19 million bowlers own their own balls.

✎ More than 14 million bowlers own their own shoes.

NOTE: Of these bowling-ball-owning adults, 1,444,314 have not gone bowling in the past year, and 3,287,714 have bowled fewer than 10 times in that same period. Look for some of these dusty balls when you stop at your next garage sale.

30

THE
UNOFFICIAL
U.S.
CENSUS

Racial Demographics in Sports

Professional sports are seen by many disadvantaged Americans as "the way out" of their poor economic circumstances. The Unofficial Census explored the role of blacks in professional sports.

While a majority of players in the National Basketball Association are black (266 of the league's 354 players), the administrative staff presents a very different picture.

Of the league's 72 head and assistant coaches, only 20 are black.

NOTE: The National Football League also employs a majority of black players (60 percent). Just 17 percent of Major League Baseball players, however, are black. An additional 13 percent are Latin or Hispanic.

Counting America's Minority Golfers

A great deal of attention has been focused recently on the issue of "exclusive golf clubs." Many of these clubs, either explicitly or implicitly, exclude people of certain races or religions. The Unofficial Census explored this divisive issue.

As we learned, there are more than 23 million golfers in America.

Of these fanatics, 1,782,647 belong to private golf clubs.

Of this privileged number, 535 are black.

NOTE: In the face of golf's restrictive history, the number of black golfers has grown substantially over recent years, to 692,000 today. African-Americans are not the only minority group that faces discrimination at our nation's golf clubs. Even though they comprise 23 percent of America's golfers, women are often restricted from playing at certain times.

Short Basketball Players—Number Playing Professionally

Basketball is thought of as a tall person's game. In reality, however, a small number of short men have made it into basketball's elite.

Of today's 354 players in the NBA, 8 are under 6 feet tall.

Counting Baseball's Millionaires

Major league sports are viewed by many as an easy route to prosperity. But how many Americans actually make millions playing professional sports? The Unofficial Census looked at this issue within the arena of professional baseball.

As we discovered, only a few Americans are making their millions playing baseball. What we also discovered, however, is that a large percentage of those who do make the big leagues become million-dollar players.

Of the 735 baseball players on major league rosters, 162 earn more than $1,000,000 each year.

Interestingly, almost as many of these professionals, 130 players, will earn the league's minimum annual salary of $100,000.

NOTE: Both the number of baseball's million-dollar players and "minimum wage earners" have increased this year, from 106 and 91 respectively. The average salary of a professional baseball player is $586,816, an increase of nearly 20 percent from last year's figure.

Richest Americans— Description

Every year, *Forbes* magazine lists the nation's 400 richest residents. The Unofficial Census explored the backgrounds of these "filthy rich" Americans.

Of these billionaires and millionaires, all had wealth in excess of $260 million.

Just over half, 211, made their money on their own. The others either inherited their wealth or built their fortunes upon large inheritances.

The largest number, 60, made their fortunes in real estate. The next largest numbers made their fortunes in finance, media, oil, and manufacturing.

The largest number live in New York (74), followed by California (64), and Texas (31).

Baseball Players—
Utilization of
Smokeless Tobacco

Everyone has seen a baseball player chewing smokeless tobacco—or maybe even spitting the product into the air. The Unofficial Census turned its sights on the prevalence of this habit among our nation's professional baseball players.

Our research findings indicate that, of the nation's 650 active professional baseball players, more than a third, 254, use smokeless tobacco.

Frighteningly, 117 of these player/chewers have potentially cancerous lesions on their lips or mouths.

NOTE: Snuff is the preferred type of smokeless tobacco used by today's baseball elite (favored by almost 3 to 1 over the coarser chewing tobacco). Smokeless tobacco use is known to increase the risk of oral cancer by 400 percent.

Smokeless Tobacco Use

While most of us only encounter smokeless tobacco when we watch a baseball game, it is actually used by more than 7 million Americans, the vast majority, 6,319,405, being men.

According to our research findings, Americans favor the following types of smokeless tobacco:

TYPE OF SMOKELESS TOBACCO	NUMBER OF MEN USING
Chewing tobacco	3,560,284
Snuff	2,759,220

NOTE: The use of smokeless tobacco is greatest among men 18 to 24 years of age, and residents of Southern states. It is least likely to be found in the mouths of Northeasterners. What's more, it is estimated that 1.7 million boys aged 12 to 17 years have used smokeless tobacco within the past year. These "child chewers" consume 26 million containers of smokeless tobacco each year. A surprising 466,965 women use snuff, and 280,179 chew tobacco.

Smokers, by Population and Marital Status

✎ 52,531,200 American adults continue to smoke cigarettes.

✎ A slight majority of these smokers, 28,037,233, are men, while 24,493,967 are women.

✎ Smoking is much more pervasive among separated and divorced persons, with 45.1 percent of separated or divorced men smoking, compared with 28.7 percent of those who are married. Similarly, 38.9 percent of separated or divorced women smoke, compared with just 24.2 percent of their married counterparts.

THE
UNOFFICIAL
U.S.
CENSUS

Counting Child Smokers

While the country's health officials are deeply concerned about America's addiction to cigarettes, they are most concerned about the practice among the nation's children.

The Unofficial Census learned that 3,227,000 children under the age of 18 smoke.

A surprising number of these young smokers, 117,560, are under the age of 12.

NOTE: Children under the age of 18 consume 947 million packs of cigarettes each year. The average age for first time use of cigarettes is 13, and an astonishing 11 percent of boys and 8.5 percent of girls who smoke begin doing so in the fourth grade.

The Desire to Quit Among Smokers

On the bright side of America's smoking dilemma is the number of Americans who say they want to quit.

Our research reveals that a majority of current smokers, 44,606,560, want to quit smoking.

In fact, 17,300,000 of those who say they want to "repent for their sins" will quit for at least one day this year.

Unfortunately, only 1,300,000 of these optimists will be able to abstain for more than one year.

NOTE: It is reported that fewer than 10 percent of smokers who attempt to quit use any product or service to help them reach their goal. Of those who seek help, most frequently used aids are: smoking-cessation programs; medications; vitamins; and self-help kits. Other more obscure methods include: hypnosis (used by 363,000) and acupuncture (used by 31,500).

Prevalence of Alternative Smoking Methods

While we know that more than 52 million Americans smoke cigarettes, few people are aware of the widespread use of so-called "alternative smoking methods." The Unofficial Census, always in search of the underside of American life, turned its attention to this smoky matter.

As we discovered, a large number of Americans continue to smoke pipes and cigars:

✎ Pipes are smoked by 3,026,241 men.
✎ Cigars are smoked by 4,717,376 men.

NOTE: Not surprisingly, the heaviest users of pipes and cigars are men 45 to 64 years of age. While nearly 2.5 billion cigars were sold in the United States last year, that number represents a decline of 73 percent from the mid-1960s. Fewer than 100,000 women indulge themselves with either of these "alternative smokes."

Pilots, Distribution by Degree of Alcohol Abuse

A great deal of attention has been paid recently to the widespread problem of drunk driving in America. The Unofficial Census set out to count the prevalence of alcohol abuse and drunk driving among our nation's pilots.

Alarmingly, 10,000 of today's active pilots have been convicted of drunk driving.

Further, 1,200 of our active commercial airline pilots have been treated for alcoholism.

NOTE: Given this information from the Unofficial Census, it comes as no surprise that 25 million Americans have a severe fear of flying.

Looking at Teetotalers

According to our recent count, there are 14.5 million problem drinkers in America.

On the more restrained side of this equation, there are a much larger number of Americans, 67,488,000, who completely abstain from drinking alcohol ("teetotalers").

NOTE: Since 1980, sales of hard liquor, beer, and wine have declined steadily. Perhaps as a result of the country's increased emphasis on health and fitness, along with a growing stigma toward drinking, the number of American "teetotalers" has increased by 28 percent over the past ten years. Not surprisingly, the South is the leader in this area, with only 52 percent of its residents ever "partaking of spirits."

Counting Sexually Abstinent Americans

The Unofficial Census considered the sexual habits of American adults.

Our findings reveal that a surprisingly large number of Americans, 40,310,400, have been sexually abstinent during the past twelve months.

NOTE: Abstinent Americans are more likely to be female, older, less educated, and from Western or New England states.

Masturbation and Other Sexual Behaviors in American Adults

The Unofficial Census revealed the following information regarding the sexual practices of American adults:

SEXUAL ACT	NUMBER PRACTICING
Masturbation	160,512,000
Oral sex	155,040,000
Sadomasochistic sex	10,944,000
Sexual contact with animals	9,120,000

NOTE: American men are more likely to masturbate and receive oral sex. Both sexes are equally likely to engage in S&M, and to have sexual contact with animals.

Counting Users
of Pornography

Pornography is pervasive in today's society, and has become the focus of heated debates between religious groups and freedom of speech advocates. The Unofficial Census explored the issue of pornography use in America.

As our findings indicate, 141,031,064 American adults have been exposed to "depictions of sexually explicit material" (pornography).

Interestingly, only a slight majority of America's pornography users, 75,656,026, are men, while the remaining 65,375,038 are women.

Married Americans, by Place or Means of First Meeting

With nearly 56 million married couples populating the country, the question that comes to mind is—where did all of these people meet? We turned our attention to this romantic question.

As the following table illustrates, America's married couples met in a wide variety of settings and ways:

PLACE OR MEANS	NUMBER OF COUPLES MEETING THERE
Social situations (parties, bars, etc.)	11,130,000
School	10,573,500
Work	7,234,500
Churches/synagogues	1,669,500
Blind dates	1,669,500
Public transportation	1,113,000
Health clubs	556,500
Personal ads	556,500

Sexual Activities of Married Americans

The expression "the honeymoon is over" implies that the excitement of marriage ends with the couple's return from the honeymoon trip. The Unofficial Census couldn't resist the urge to consider the sexual state of married Americans.

As the following table illustrates, "the honeymoon" isn't over yet for a large number of married Americans:

SEXUAL ACTIVITY	NUMBER ENGAGING IN
Take showers/baths together	43,407,000
Go to hotels to be alone	37,842,000
Watch X-rated videos	24,486,000
Make love outdoors	24,000,000

Figuring Fidelity in Married Americans

The Unofficial Census discovered the following facts about the chastity of America's 55,650,000 married couples:

✎ Nearly half, 53,535,300, of America's married persons have been faithful (only had sex with their spouse).

NOTE: The country's married "faithfuls" are most likely to be female, white, less educated, live in the Midwest or New England, and reside in rural communities.

Counting Two-Timers

According to our research, at least 1,669,000 married Americans have been involved in extramarital sexual relationships during the past year.

Of these "two-timers," a certain number have been involved with the following persons:

OBJECT OF DESIRE	NUMBER HAVING SEX WITH
Close personal friend	878,157
Neighbor, co-worker, or acquaintance	411,365
Casual date or pick-up	332,397
Prostitute	31,721

NOTE: America's "cheaters" are more likely to be male, older, black, reside in the Midwest, and live in suburban communities.

Contraception, Utilization by Type and Frequency

Unwanted pregnancy and abortion have become critical issues in today's society. The Unofficial Census looked into the state of contraception use in the United States.

In our endeavor, we learned that there are 57,900,000 women of childbearing age (15 to 44) in the United States.

Of these women, 34,913,700 are currently using some form of birth control.

The following illustration depicts today's most commonly used methods of contraception:

METHOD OF CONTRACEPTION	NUMBER OF WOMEN USING
The pill	10,718,506
Sterilization	9,601,268
Condoms	5,097,400
Diaphragm	1,990,081
Periodic abstinence (rhythm)	800,000
Withdrawal	744,000
IUD	698,274
Sponge	400,000

NOTE: Of the 22,986,300 women not currently using any form of birth control, only 7 percent are at risk for unintended pregnancy. The others are either: sterilized for health reasons; sterile for other than surgical reasons; pregnant; trying to become pregnant; or sexually inactive. Still, more than 3 million women each year become pregnant unintentionally. Of these, 1.6 million receive abortions.

Sterilization as Birth Control, Incidence by Gender

With the population of the United States aging, surgical sterilization is being practiced more often by Americans in search of permanent birth control. The Unofficial Census looked into this very personal subject.

As we discovered, 13,700,000 Americans have selected sterilization as their method of birth control.

Of these Americans, a majority, 9,601,268, are women, while 4,098,732 are men.

NOTE: When males and females are taken together, sterilization becomes the nation's leading method of birth control. Offering two of the lowest risks of pregnancy (0.15% and 0.4% respectively), male and female sterilization has increased in popularity in recent years. At the same time, more Americans are using the pill and condoms. Fewer are using IUDs, diaphragms, and the sponge.

Counting Sex Instructors

While a vast majority of America's adults favor sex education in the schools, a small, but very vocal, minority has made that goal more difficult to achieve. Regardless of the obstacles, however, a majority of states now require sex education in their schools. The Unofficial Census investigated who was teaching this "new" subject.

As we discovered, few sex education instructors are specialists in this area. In most cases, the schools have called upon teachers from loosely related subject areas to cover this topic.

The following table illustrates the professional specialization of today's 111,500 sex education instructors:

Area of Specialization	Number Teaching Sex Ed
Physical education	34,565
Health education	28,990
Home economics	25,645
Biology	18,955
Nursing	3,345

Elementary School Teachers—Distribution by Favorite Apples

Apples are among America's favorite fruits. Each American consumes more than 20 pounds of apples each year. The apple is also the traditional gift for a young student to give his teacher. The Unofficial Census looked into apple consumption preferences among America's elementary school teachers.

As the following table illustrates, America's 1.5 million elementary school teachers have strong preferences when it comes to apples:

Type of Apple	Number of Teachers Preferring
Red delicious	585,000
Golden delicious	360,000
Granny Smith	300,000
McIntosh	150,000

Counting America's One Room Schools

When most people think of one room schools, they probably think back to the days of Tom Sawyer and Huckleberry Finn. In reality, however, one room schools are still alive and well, and functioning in large numbers.

There are 1,279 one room schools operating today. These schools have an average of 20 students each and, when taken all together, are the educational setting for more than 25,000 children.

Half of America's one room schools, 639, are operating under the auspices of public school districts. The remaining number are operated privately.

Not surprisingly, the largest number of one room schools are found in less populated states. The largest number, 322, can be found in Nebraska. The next largest number are located in: Pennsylvania, 257; Montana, 111; South Dakota, 94; and Ohio, 84.

Schoolchildren, by Number Educated at Home

Home schooling has become a battleground between government and school officials on the one side, and religious groups and personal rights advocates on the other. The Unofficial Census counted the number of children who are educated at home.

As our count reveals, at least 300,000 of the nation's 46 million school-age children are being educated at home.

Of these kids, a majority, 218,000, score one year or more above their grade level in reading. An additional 149,000 score one year or more above their grade level in math.

Also discovered in our count was the fact that 46,000 home-schooled children are "underground" from the authorities, refusing to comply with state and local regulations.

NOTE: Some sources put the number of home-schooled children at as many as 1 million. Regardless of the source, the number of home-educated children has increased dramatically in recent years. While traditionally home schooling has been only practiced for religious reasons, a broader group of parents has opted against traditional public or parochial schooling.

Americans—
Distribution by
Amount of Education

The Unofficial Census counted America's adults by the
amount of formal education they have received:

✎ At latest count, more than 350,000 American adults
have received no formal education.
✎ Additionally, 3.2 million adults have not completed the
sixth grade.

On this question's more educated extreme, 5.3 million
Americans have received more than 18 years of formal education (6 or more years of college and graduate school).

Bicyclists, by Use of Protective Helmets

Bicycle riding is America's third most popular participation sport, following swimming and exercise walking. More than 90 million Americans ride bicycles.

Unfortunately, only a small percentage of these riders, fewer than 9 million persons, use protective helmets.

NOTE: Child cyclists are least likely to wear helmets, with only 2 percent of kids using the protective wear. Given the fact that 1 child dies and 200 are treated in emergency rooms each day from bicycle-related head injuries, it is very surprising that only 5 percent of the 2 million kids who will receive bicycles as gifts each year will also receive helmets.

Motorcycle Demographics

While the number of motorcycles has dwindled by more than 1 million over the past few years, there are still a large number of "two-wheelers" rolling along our nation's roads.

As we discovered, there are 4,209,000 registered motorcycles in use in America today.

There are more than 5 million Americans who say they ride these vehicles.

Surprisingly, 553,850 of these adventurous Americans are over 50 years old.

NOTE: Our nation's motorcyclists have formed a number of special interest organizations including: the Christian Motorcyclists Association (33,000 members); the Wheelchair Motorcycle Association (1,000 members); and the Alliance of Women Bikers (300 members).

Cars, Distribution by Age

There is nothing like the smell of a new car interior, or at least that's what we've always been told. The Unofficial Census researched the agedness of America's fleet.

As the following chart reveals, relatively few Americans are smelling that "new car smell":

Age of Car	Number on Road
Less than 1 year	7,812,000
1–5 years	47,569,500
5–10 years	42,687,000
10–15 years	27,760,500
15 years or older	13,671,000

NOTE: The average car in the United States is 7.6 years old, older than the averages of 6.59 years recorded in 1980, and 5.55 years recorded in 1970.

Cars, Distribution by Those With/ Without Tops

The Unofficial Census counted the number of Americans who own convertible automobiles.

As our findings indicate, of the 139,500,000 car-owning Americans, only 112,000 own convertibles.

NOTE: While sales of convertibles have been growing steadily since 1982, ownership levels have not come close to the all-time high of 540,000 set in 1963.

Car Owners— Distribution by Number Doing Own Maintenance

A majority of Americans do at least some minor maintenance on their automobiles. The Unofficial Census counted America's 139,500,000 car owners by their participation in certain automobile upkeep.

As the following table illustrates, the number of Americans involved in maintaining their cars varies widely by the task:

Maintenance Work	Number Doing Themselves
Pump gas	108,810,000
Change oil	65,565,000
Change oil filter	46,593,000
Change spark plugs	33,340,500
Install new battery	18,972,000
Install new shock absorbers	15,903,000
Install mufflers	6,556,500

NOTE: The number of Americans who pump their own gas has grown dramatically, from just 17 percent in 1975, to 78 percent today, with the increase in self-service gas stations.

Cars—Frequency and Method of Bathing

To most Americans, their car represents their second largest financial investment after their home. The Unofficial Census decided to investigate the degree to which Americans keep their cars clean.

As our research revealed, 34,177,500 of America's 139,500,000 cars are washed at least once each week.

On the dirtier side of this question, 6,556,500 cars are never washed.

Seat Belts, by
Frequency of Use

Every American has heard about the importance of using their seat belt. But how many Americans have taken this sage advice? The Unofficial Census counted the number of safe ("smart") and unsafe ("reckless") Americans.

According to our findings, a majority of American adults, 119,472,000 persons, use seat belts.

A significant number, however, only use seat belts occasionally. 39,216,000 Americans fall into this precarious category.

Further, a large minority of Americans, 20,976,000, never use seat belts.

NOTE: An estimated 15,900 highway deaths could be prevented by seat belts each year—if they were used. Fortunately, 84 percent of parents are now using safety seats for their infants and toddlers, more than three times the number using them in 1981.

Seat Belt Nonusers, by Reason for Abstinence

While a vast majority of adults, 89 percent, consider driving a car to be a risky activity, 33 percent do not always use seat belts.

These 60,192,000 "reckless" Americans blamed the following circumstances for their behavior:

REASON FOR NOT WEARING SEAT BELT	NUMBER CLAIMING
Haven't thought about it	23,474,880
They're uncomfortable	20,465,280
Want to be able to get out quickly in an accident	20,465,280
Too much bother	16,853,760
Careful driver	10,834,560
Not necessary for short trips	9,028,800
Not effective in a serious accident	8,426,880
Won't have an accident	7,824,960
Car, life and health are insured	6,019,200
Car doesn't have seat belts	3,611,520

NOTE: A larger percentage of male, young, rural, and poor Americans consider seat belts to be optional equipment.

Gamblers—Distribution by Preferred Games of Chance

A majority of Americans, 71 percent, gamble. While most of these individuals place their bets on legalized state lotteries, a large number bet illegally, and with better odds, on privately organized games of chance.

As the following table illustrates, American adults risk their money on the outcomes of a variety of events:

GAME	NUMBER WAGERING ON OUTCOME
State lotteries	98,496,000
Card games	41,952,000
Professional sports	40,128,000
Casino games	36,480,000
The numbers	32,832,000
College sports	25,536,000
Horse races	25,536,000
Bingo	23,712,000
Boxing	14,592,000
Dog races	10,944,000
Jai-alai	5,472,000

NOTE: Americans wager more than $241 billion each year. That comes to nearly $1,000 for every man, woman, and child. More than two-thirds of this money, $161.9 billion, is risked in casinos while only 7 percent, $17.1 billion, is spent on lottery tickets.

Gamblers— Distribution by Attitudes on Game-Fixing

There have been a number of recent sports scandals that have focused renewed attention on the issue of criminal involvement in organized sports. The Unofficial Census counted our nation's gamblers by their feelings on this subject.

As the following table illustrates, a majority of gamblers believe that at least some of the outcomes of certain sporting events are fixed:

Sporting Event	Number Believe Fixing Occurs
Boxing	91,947,840
Horse racing	86,767,680
Professional football	69,932,160
College sports	66,047,040
Professional basketball	64,752,000
Major league baseball	62,161,920

Gamblers— Distribution by Reasons for Behavior

With 129,504,000 American adults describing themselves as gamblers, the Unofficial Census decided to explore the underlying reasons behind this behavior.

As the following table illustrates, America's gamblers give a variety of reasons for their behavior:

REASON FOR GAMBLING	NUMBER AGREEING
Recreation	50,506,560
Make money/get rich	34,966,080
Excitement	15,540,480
Challenge	14,245,440
Social activity	7,770,240
Make game more interesting	5,180,160

NOTE: America's gamblers are more likely to be male, white, urban, and wealthy.

Gamblers— Distribution by Current Financial Standing

With Americans wagering total amounts of money larger than the GNPs of many countries, the issue that naturally comes to mind is how many of these gamblers are winners. The Unofficial Census counted the winners—and the losers.

The following table reveals the financial standing of America's gamblers:

FINANCIAL POSITION	NUMBER CLAIMING
Ahead	31,080,960
Behind	75,112,320
Even	19,425,600

NOTE: There are an estimated 15 million compulsive gamblers in the United States.

Looking at Beautiful Americans

It is often said that people "are their own worst critics." Is this saying true or is it just another myth? The Unofficial Census turned its attention to this narcissistic question.

The following table illustrates the way American adults assess their own physical appearances:

DESCRIPTION	NUMBER DESCRIBING THEMSELVES THIS WAY
Extremely attractive	7,296,000
Very attractive	19,152,000
Pretty or handsome	37,392,000
Average	72,960,000
"Interesting" looking	20,976,000
Plain	9,120,000

NOTE: Interestingly, a greater proportion of women label themselves as having "average looks," while a larger number of men consider themselves to be "plain."

T H E
UNOFFICIAL
U.S.
CENSUS

Counting Women's Bodies, by Dress Size

The Unofficial Census learned the following about the dress sizes of America's women:

Dress Size	Number of Women Wearing
4–6	9,339,291
8–10	28,017,873
12–14	29,885,732
16 or larger	23,348,228

Counting Women's Feet, by Shoe Size

The Unofficial Census learned the following about the foot sizes of America's women:

Shoe Size	Number of Women Wearing
5– 5½	4,669,646
6– 6½	14,008,937
7– 7½	25,216,086
8– 8½	27,083,944
9– 9½	13,075,008
10–10½	6,537,504

High Heel Shoes—
Number and Reasons
for Wearing

It has often been said—by women—that high heel shoes were invented by a man. The discomfort that these shoes inflict can be understood by a simple look at their construction. The Unofficial Census looked at this painful, yet fashionable, subject in greater detail.

As we discovered, a majority of American women, 57 million, wear high heels. Of these, 55 million wear them regularly. These figures are surprising in light of the fact that most women find high heels to be more uncomfortable than any other shoes. Women offer a variety of reasons for their wearing high heels:

REASON FOR WEARING HIGH HEELS	NUMBER CITING
To be in fashion	34,714,145
To look slimmer	28,101,927
To look more attractive to men	22,591,745
To look taller	22,591,745

NOTE: Despite the fact that a majority of Americans report having sore feet, 45 percent of women, and 20 percent of men, wear shoes that are uncomfortable but look good on their feet.

High Heel Shoes—
Places More
Likely Worn

With nearly 57 million women wearing high heels, the Unofficial Census asked the following question—to what events are women most likely to wear these uncomfortable shoes?

The following chart answers this often asked question:

PLACES HIGH HEELS WORN	NUMBER CITING
Weddings	45,575,741
Out to dinner	37,599,986
Parties	36,460,592
Job interviews	34,751,502
Dancing	29,624,231
Theater or movie	22,787,870
Work	18,230,296
On way to work	17,090,903
Entertaining at home	15,951,509
Shopping	10,254,542

America's Feet— Number Having Been Seen by a Podiatrist

More than 18 million Americans (having 36 million feet), have called on a podiatrist for the treatment of their foot problems. As the following table illustrates, these unfortunate Americans were driven to seek professional consultation by a variety of ailments:

COMPLAINT	NUMBER CITING
Sore, aching feet	7,113,600
Ingrown toenails	5,107,200
Corns	4,377,600
Warts/Plantar warts	3,830,400
Calluses	3,283,200

U.S. Breast Size Clusters

Much attention is paid to the size of women's breasts. "Too much attention," say many. The question that comes all too naturally to the Unofficial Census is, how many women have small, medium, and large breasts? We went out in active search of some answers to these sizeable questions.

According to our findings, American women report having the following size breasts:

Breast Size	Number Possessing
Small	25,644,870
Average	44,641,070
Large	18,046,390

NOTE: While the largest number of women say that they have average-sized breasts, an even larger number, 50 percent, believe that men find large breasts most attractive.

Another Look at Breasts, by Bra Size

America's women wear the following bra sizes:

Bra Size	Number Wearing
AAA–A	11,029,703
B	35,741,467
C	30,175,250
D	11,926,275
DD +	4,333,431

Counting America's Breasts, by Number Having Implants

Always in search of statistics which communicate the undercurrents of American life, the Unofficial Census set out to examine a growing national trend, breast implantation.

As we discovered, more than 2 million American women have received breast implants.

Interestingly, only 400,000 of these women received their implants following surgery for breast cancer.

The remaining "implantees," 1.6 million women, received them for other reasons.

NOTE: 150,000 American women receive breast implants each year. Nearly 40 percent of these women will suffer from complications, some of them serious.

Male Chests—
Distribution by
Degree of forestation

America's men have chests of the following description:

Chest Type	Number of Men Having
Smooth	41,833,332
Hairy	37,382,977

NOTE: While a greater number of men have smooth chests, most men believe that women prefer hairy-chested men.

THE
UNOFFICIAL
U.S.
CENSUS

Male Shoulders—
Distribution by Size

America's men have shoulders of the following description:

	NUMBER OF
SHOULDER TYPE	MEN HAVING
Medium	52,514,183
Broad	23,141,843

NOTE: While a large majority of American men have medium-size shoulders, nearly one-half of men believe that women like broad-shouldered men better.

Male Facial Hair—Incidence

One in four American men, 22,251,772, have mustaches. A fewer number, 8,010,638, have beards. Nearly 10 million have both.

NOTE: Our hairy-faced citizens are more likely to be younger and reside in the Northeast or the South.

T H E
UNOFFICIAL
U.S.
CENSUS

Counting Bald, and Balding, Heads

Nearly one-third of American men, 26,500,000, are bald or have significant hair loss.

On the more feminine side of this revealing issue, nearly 24 million women have thinning hair.

Gray Hair—Number of Men Coloring

An estimated 40 million American men have gray hair.

Of these "distinguished gentlemen," 3,200,000 choose to cover their gray with hair coloring.

Gray Hair—Number of Women Coloring

More than 37 million American women color their hair. Of these changers, more than 13 million use hair coloring to cover gray.

Women, by Current Hair Color

It is often said that "blondes have more fun." While this may or may not be true, it led the Unofficial Census to consider the question of hair color in American women.

As the following table illustrates, American women report having the following hair color in the greatest numbers:

Hair Color	Women Having
Red	5,603,575
Blonde	15,876,795
Brunette (Black/Brown)	62,573,251

NOTE: While the largest number of women have brown hair, it is not surprising that most women, 60 percent, believe that men find blonde hair most attractive. Strangely, only 19 percent of women (just slightly more than the 17 percent who have blonde hair) say that they would most like to have blonde hair.

Sensual Women— Distribution by Hair Color

A majority of American women consider themselves to be sensual. The following table illustrates the number of women, as distinguished by their hair color, who consider themselves sensual:

Hair Color	Number Who Are Sensual	%
Redheads	4,202,681	75
Brunettes	46,304,206	74
Blondes	10,319,917	65

THE UNOFFICIAL U.S. CENSUS

Flirtatious Women—
Distribution by
Hair Color

$\mathbf{A}$ majority of American women consider themselves to be flirtatious. The following table illustrates how many of America's women, as denoted by their hair color, consider themselves flirts:

Hair Color	Number Who Are Flirts	%
Blondes	13,336,508	84
Redheads	3,586,288	64
Brunettes	33,163,823	53

Self-Confident Women—Distribution by Hair Color

A majority of American women consider themselves to be self-confident. The following table illustrates how many American women, as defined by their hair color, are self-confident:

Hair Color	Number Who Are Self-Confident	%
Redheads	3,978,538	71
Brunettes	40,672,613	65
Blondes	7,462,094	47

Popular Women—
Distribution by
Hair Color

A majority of American women believe that they are popular with men. The following table illustrates the number of women, as categorized by their hair color, who feel they are attractive to the opposite sex:

Hair Color	Number Attractive To Men	%
Blondes	14,447,883	91
Brunettes	46,304,206	74
Redheads	3,586,288	64

Blondes, by Number
Having "More Fun"

It is widely suggested that "blondes have more fun." But is this really true or is it just another one of our many myths?

As our research reveals, and the myth correctly alleges, blondes are indeed more likely to have "more fun." A majority of America's blondes, 11,748,828, report that they have more fun.

On the other side of this heated question, however, are a majority of non-blondes, 65 percent, who contend that they, and not blondes, are the ones having more fun.

Expressions, by Number Believing in Their Wisdom

We are often told that something is "just an expression." This implies that the saying has no validity or value. The Unofficial Census looked at our popular expressions in greater detail.

As we learned, a large number of American adults believe in many of today's, and yesterday's, most popular expressions:

Popular Saying	Number Believing It's True	%
Look Before You Leap	175,104,000	96
Don't Count Your Chickens Before . . .	169,632,000	93
Don't Cry Over Spilled Milk	160,512,000	88
Don't Put All Your Eggs in One Basket	158,688,000	87
A Penny Saved is a Penny Earned	155,040,000	85
Haste Makes Waste	153,216,000	84
Beauty Is Only Skin Deep	149,568,000	82
A Stitch in Time Saves Nine	142,272,000	78
The Early Bird Catches the Worm	136,800,000	75
A Bird in the Hand Is Worth . . .	133,152,000	73
What's Good for the Goose Is Good . . .	103,968,000	57
The Grass Is Always Greener . . .	69,312,000	38

Pet Peeves— Distribution by Number of Complainers

Every American knows of something that "just drives them crazy." The Unofficial Census counted Americans by their most commonly mentioned "pet peeves."

As the following table illustrates, American adults hold very strong opinions regarding the things that they find bothersome:

PET PEEVE	NUMBER CITING
People talking during movies	156,864,000
Long supermarket lines	153,216,000
People blowing horns in traffic	145,920,000
Paying to see a bad movie	134,976,000
TV commercials	131,328,000
People smoking in restaurants	124,032,000

Certain Unethical Behaviors, by Number Practicing

We have all had someone push in front of us while we are waiting in line. But how prevalent is this problem and how does it compare in its frequency to other ethical lapses? The Unofficial Census explored these rude questions.

As we discovered, 34,672,150 Americans cut into lines.

Surprisingly, however, this number is much smaller than the 74,818,850 Americans who sometimes drive while drunk.

Furs, by Number Wearing and Boycotting

One of today's most heated arguments focuses on the wearing of fur. Fur owners fight for their freedom to choose, while animal rights advocates voice their concerns over the sometimes brutal practice of fur trapping.

The Fur Information Council (an industry trade group) claims that more than 30 million Americans continue to wear fur. Of these, nearly 7 million are men.

As we also learned, however, more than 10 million Americans are actively boycotting fur. This number represents a fourfold increase over the number doing so in 1984.

NOTE: Judging from the decreasing number of animals trapped each year, animal rights advocates seem to be having an impact on fur sales.

Hunters, by Number of Participants and Kills

America's hunters are a committed group. Their hunting licenses alone cost more than $400 million each year. The Unofficial Census took a closer look at our nation's "happy hunters."

As our research reveals, there are 15,858,063 licensed hunters in the United States. The total number of hunters exceeds 20 million persons.

The greatest number of licensed hunters hail from the following states: Texas (1,189,077); Pennsylvania (1,174,424); Michigan (938,503); and New York (757,897).

Our nation's hunters kill more than 200 million animals each year including: 25 million rabbits; 22 million squirrels; 4.6 million deer; 350,000 wild turkeys; and 22,000 bears.

Gun Ownership— Women

Firearms have traditionally been looked upon as "manly toys." But with the petite likes of Nancy Reagan packing a pistol, the Unofficial Census decided to attempt a count of the country's gun-toting women.

As our count reveals, a growing percentage of the country's gun owners are women. Approximately 23 million women in the United States own firearms. These women own an arsenal that includes: 12 million handguns, 13 million shotguns, and 14 million rifles.

Guns, by
Number Loaded

Firearms are deadly instruments. This statement remains true, however, only when they are loaded. The Unofficial Census set out to count the number of loaded guns in America.

At last count, there were 60 million guns in America.

Of these weapons, approximately one-third are kept loaded by their owners.

Counting Latchkey Kids in Homes With Guns

More and more American women are entering the workforce. At the same time, the number of two-career couples with children is increasing at a rapid pace. As a result, the number of elementary school–age children who are left alone after school (latchkey kids) has grown to 2,790,000.

Bearing in mind the large number of firearms owned by Americans, the Unofficial Census turned a watchful eye toward the issue of latchkey kids who are left alone in gun-owning homes.

As our worst suspicions bear out, a large number of these kids, 1,227,600, are left unsupervised in homes containing firearms.

Given the most current data on firearms, one-third of these weapons, more than 400,000, are kept loaded.

NOTE: An average of 4 Americans are killed accidentally by firearms each day. Of these innocent victims, at least 1 is a child under the age of 15.

Flag Wavers—
Distribution by Age

A great deal of heated debate has been focused recently on the issue of flag-burning. With military veterans and conservative Americans on the one side, and civil libertarians on the other, the flag, a symbol of the United States, has also become a symbol of the fight for freedom of speech. The Unofficial Census counted this nation's flag wavers.

An estimated 9,120,000 Americans fly the flag in front of their homes at least once each week.

As might be expected, older Americans are more than twice as likely to make this expression as their younger counterparts.

Counting Our Army, The Salvation Army

Everyone has seen Salvation Army "bell ringers" asking for charitable contributions during the holiday season. The Unofficial Census asked the following questions: why is this organization called an "army"; does it subscribe to military rankings; and how many troops does it have deployed?

As we learned, the Salvation Army is actually a Christian organization run by men and women who have dedicated their lives to serving God. The group is run by 5,025 ministers who go by military rankings.

The highest rank, General, is held by just one person. Other ranks include Commissioner, Colonel, Lieutenant Colonel, Major, Captain, and Lieutenant.

The army also counts 40,000 "non-commissioned" employees among its forces. More than 1.2 million volunteers complete the deployment.

NOTE: The Salvation Army helps more than 26 million Americans each year. The Army is also working to help disadvantaged persons in 90 other countries.

THE
UNOFFICIAL
U.S.
CENSUS

Counting Our
Space Travelers

It is a persistent long-term dream of millions of Americans to visit outer space. But how many of us have actually realized that dream and who are these space travelers? The Unofficial Census looked into these galactic questions.

Our research reveals the fact that only 173 individuals have earned the title of United States Astronaut since the creation of that job title in 1959.

What's more, only two-thirds of America's astronauts have actually gone into space.

NOTE: It has been reported that during the last selection of astronauts held in 1987, nearly 2,000 applicants competed for just 15 openings. Clearly, this American dream is still alive and well. Interestingly, 60 percent of today's astronauts are in the military, 16 percent have Ph.D.s, and 11 percent are medical doctors.

Truck Drivers— Gender Demographics

Truck drivers are most often thought of as tattoo-covered men who drive hard and eat badly. Our research, however, indicates some interesting trends in the composition of our nation's truckers.

Our findings indicate that there are more than 2,500,000 truck drivers in America.

Interestingly, more than 100,000 of these drivers are women.

NOTE: While the number of white male truck drivers has not increased over the past two years, the number of women truckers has grown by 8 percent. With a declining interest in the profession among white males, the trucking industry plans to recruit more minorities and women. "10-4 Big Gal!"

Psychiatrists, Number Having Sexual Relations With Clients

There are 33,700 psychiatrists in America.

Of these licensed professionals, 977 have had sex with at least one client while that person was in their care.

NOTE: Earlier surveys have shown that as many as 2,300 psychotherapists have had sexual relations with a patient. In the past five years, at least 7 states have made sex between a psychotherapist and a patient a felony. Other states are currently considering similar legislation.

Priests—Number True to Their Vows of Celibacy

Of this country's 57,317 priests, all have taken a vow of celibacy. The Unofficial Census decided to count how many of these "Fathers" have remained true to this pledge.

Our research indicates that half of America's priests, 28,659, have broken their celibacy vows and are sexually active.

America's wayward priests are currently involved in the following sexual activities:

SEXUAL ACTIVITY	NUMBER OF PRIESTS INVOLVED
Heterosexual sex	16,049
Homosexual sex	5,732
Sex with minors	3,439
Frequent ("problematic") masturbation	2,866
Transvestism	573

NOTE: Mandatory celibacy is a major reason for men leaving the priesthood. It is estimated that the number of priests in the United States will decline by nearly 40 percent by the year 2000. Meanwhile, the number of U.S. Catholics has continued to grow.

Lawyers, by Degree of Happiness

The number of lawyers in America has continued to grow. At last count, there were 724,000 lawyers populating the country. The Unofficial Census counted the number of lawyers who are happy with their choice of profession.

As we discovered, nearly 240,000 lawyers say they are "very satisfied" with their jobs. This number represents a 20 percent decline from 1984's figure.

As evidence of this decreasing job satisfaction, the number of lawyers who consume 6 or more drinks each day has grown to 94,000 (more than 1 in 8), a dramatic increase from the 3,500 lawyers who admitted to this behavior in 1984.

The Incidence of Depressed Americans in Certain Professions

Most Americans feel depressed from time to time. But how many Americans suffer from serious depression, and are workers in certain professions more likely to be victims? The Unofficial Census pursued this intriguing question.

As our research reveals, depression affects more than 10 million Americans each year. Further, certain professions do employ a higher percentage of depressed individuals. The following table illustrates the wide range of depression rates among a sampling of professions.

Profession	Number Employed	Number Depressed	%
Data-entry keyers	414,000	53,820	13
Typists	731,000	73,100	10
Lawyers	741,000	74,100	10
Waiters & Waitresses	1,389,000	111,120	8
Secretaries	4,010,000	280,700	7
Hairdresser/Cosmetologists	736,000	51,520	7
Writers/Artists/Entertainers/Athletes	1,921,000	115,260	6

NOTE: The question remains whether certain professions are more likely to cause depression, or that they tend to attract a greater number of depressed workers. Some of the professions showing little or no depression include computer programmers and auto mechanics. As a point of reference, between 3 and 5 percent of the general population is depressed.

Profession	Number Employed	Number Depressed	%
Bank Tellers	503,000	30,180	6
Elementary school teachers	1,489,000	74,450	5
Accountants/Auditors	1,416,000	70,800	5
Truck drivers	1,850,000	74,000	4
Registered nurses	1,599,000	63,960	4
Receptionists	815,000	24,450	3
Executives/Managers	14,848,000	565,440	3
Cooks	1,713,000	34,260	2

Depressed Americans, by Method of Response

7,296,000 adults claim that they never get depressed. The remaining, less fortunate, Americans ease their feelings of depression through participation in a number of activities. The following chart illustrates some of the most commonly used aids:

ACTIVITY	NUMBER OF DEPRESSED ADULTS PRACTICING
Telephone a friend	77,045,760
Get together with friends	63,037,440
Watch television	59,535,360
Listen to music	50,780,160
Read	42,000,000
Examine feelings	42,024,960
Pray	42,024,960
Eat	38,522,880
Sleep	35,000,000
Clean house	35,000,000

NOTE: More women than men prefer to face their depression by telephoning or seeing friends, reading, or praying. A greater number of men prefer to deal with their depression by watching television.

Walking—Rank by Profession

The average American walks more than 50,000 miles over the course of his or her lifetime. The Unofficial Census analyzed the amount of walking required in certain professions.

As the following table illustrates, certain professions tend to require a greater amount of walking from their employees:

PROFESSION	AVG. MILES WALKED	
	DAY	YEAR
Police	6.8	1,632
Mail Carriers	4.4	1,056
TV Reporters	4.2	1,008
Nurses	3.9	942
Doctors	3.5	840
Retail Salespeople	3.4	804
Secretaries	3.3	792
Actors	3.2	776
Public Relations Personnel	2.7	666
Real Estate Agents	2.6	622
TV Producers	2.1	517
Newspaper Reporters	2.0	476
Homemakers	1.8	433
Bankers	1.4	335
Radio Announcers	1.1	264
Lawyers	.9	210
AVERAGE	2.9	696

Mail Handlers, by Number of Dog Bite Recipients

America's postal workers often have to endure great hardship in their struggle to make sure that the mail gets through. As the postal saying goes, "Neither snow, nor rain, nor heat, nor gloom of night . . ." But, noticeably, no mention is made in this motto of another obstacle that frequently faces our nation's mail handlers, aggressive dogs.

Of the 49,937 mail handlers employed by the U.S. Postal Service, more than 3,500 will be seriously bitten by a dog this year.

Counting Dog Bite Victims and Their Attackers

Our research indicates that at least 1 million Americans are bitten by dogs each year.

Our research also reveals that approximately 11 of these victims will die.

Based on our research findings, the following breeds are most likely to be involved in fatal biting incidents:

Dog Breed	Percent of Fatal Attacks
Pit Bull Terrier	42
German Shepherd	15
Husky	12
Malamute	6
Doberman Pinscher	5
Rottweiler	5
Great Dane	4
Saint Bernard	4

NOTE: Another interesting result from our research is the fact that 16 percent of those persons killed by dog bites are children less than 1 year old. An additional 70 percent of victims are children less than 10 years old, and 10 percent are adults 70 years or older.

Counting Cat Bite Victims and Their Attackers

Contrary to popular belief, dogs are not the only American pet capable of causing physical harm. The Unofficial Census looked into this feline fact.

As our research reveals, cats are responsible for nearly 155,591 bites each year. We also learned the following about these cats and their victims:

A majority of biters, 104,246, are female.

A majority of biters, 88,687, are strays.

A majority of *victims*, 91,799, are female.

A majority of the wounds received, 108,914, are scratches. The next largest number, 42,010, are punctures, followed by 4,667 tears.

NOTE: The higher incidence of female cat bite victims may be partly explained by the higher incidence of cat ownership among women.

Punches, by Number of Recipients

As is widely known, America is a violent society. At last count, more than 1 in 3 adults, 66 million Americans, report having been punched by another human being.

While not comprising a majority of the country's victims, a surprisingly large number are women. More than 21 million American women have received a physical beating.

As the following table illustrates, Jewish adults are also more likely to have been victims of punches or beatings:

RELIGION	NUMBER PUNCHED	%
Jewish	2,354,982	53
Catholic	15,477,710	38
Protestant	20,283,946	33

NOTE: In addition to men and Jews, black Americans, younger Americans, those with more education, and residents of Western states are more likely to have been punched.

Incidence of Black Eyes and Other Injuries

It is often said that "as long as you have your health you are a lucky person." The Unofficial Census counted Americans by the number of injuries they have endured.

As the following table illustrates, the cumulative incidence of certain injuries varies widely:

CONDITION	NUMBER OF ADULTS HAVING HAD
Black eye	80,256,000
Broken arm or finger	52,896,000
Injuries from car accident	41,952,000
Broken leg or toe	38,304,000
Concussion	29,184,000

NOTE: Men are more likely than women to suffer from all of the above conditions.

Spanking—Utilization By U.S. Parents

While some consider it to be effective discipline, others call it child abuse. How many American parents spank their children and how many of these Americans believe that it works? The Unofficial Census looked into this painful issue:

✎ Our research indicates that there are 127,692,000 parents with children under the age of 18.

✎ A vast majority of these parents, 105,984,360, report that they have spanked their children.

✎ Interestingly, almost half of these spankers, 42,393,744, believe that this form of corporal punishment is seldom, if ever, effective.

NOTE: What's more, nearly 35 million of these spankers feel that they, and not their children, are responsible for the spanking. In many of these cases, parents are acting out of frustration and not out of any premeditated approval of spanking.

The Incidence
of Spanking in
American Schools

While most American parents approve of spanking at home, a majority believe that teachers should never hit children. Only 38 percent of America's teachers agree, however, raising the question of how many children are subject to corporal punishment in school? The Unofficial Census turned its sights toward this controversial subject.

Our findings indicate that 1,157,270 American children are disciplined with physical punishment in schools each year.

Of these children, nearly 20,000 are seriously injured in the process.

As we can see in the chart on the following page, the country's Southern states lead in the use of corporal punishment.

NOTE: While still permitted in schools in 30 states, corporal punishment has been outlawed in 11 states since 1987. Interestingly, the United States military banned the practice of corporal punishment in 1874. Increased litigation and the introduction of more "enlightened" disciplinary techniques are cited as two major causes for the abandonment of corporal punishment in many states.

116

State	Number of Students Spanked Each Year	%
Arkansas	59,321	13.7
Alabama	74,541	10.3
Mississippi	51,912	10.3
Tennessee	71,394	8.8
Oklahoma	46,131	7.9
Georgia	90,362	7.8
Texas	261,121	7.8
Florida	126,618	7.1
South Carolina	34,528	5.6
Louisiana	39,360	4.9
U.S. Total/Avg.	1,157,270	2.9

Crime Victims, by Reason for Not Reporting Incident to Police

Nearly 15 percent of Americans are the victim of a crime each year.

Of these 36 million unfortunate individuals, a majority, 22 million, do not report the incident to the police.

The following table details some of the reasons most commonly cited for not reporting a crime:

Reasons for Not Reporting Crime	Number Citing
The crime is not successfully completed	5,676,000
Perceived lack of proof	2,354,000
Private matter	1,606,000
No ID number on lost property	1,518,000
Police would not want to be bothered	1,430,000
Too inconvenient	748,000
Police would not be able to help	594,000
Fear of reprisal	286,000

Bullet-Proof Vests, by Number of Lives Saved

Bullet-proof vests have saved the lives of at least 1,170 Americans.

Of these lucky Americans, 527 were saved from gun-shot attacks, 468 were saved during traffic accidents, and 175 were saved from knife attacks.

NOTE: Despite the fact that their average cost is only $350, just 20 percent of the country's police officers wear bullet-proof vests.

THE
UNOFFICIAL
U.S.
CENSUS

Murder Victims, by Number and Relationship of Those Knowing

Most Americans know somebody who has been the victim of a crime, whether it was a burglary or a relatively minor assault. But how many Americans have known the victim of a murder? The Unofficial Census answered this assaulting question.

Shockingly, more than 1 out of every 10 American adults, 18,914,880 persons, knows someone who was murdered within the past year.

Of these grieving Americans, 2,379,492 were related to the victim.

Another 7,138,476 Americans were friends of murder victims, while 1,189,746 were neighbors, and 1,070,582 were co-workers.

Counting Haters

Simply hearing the term "Ku Klux Klan" (KKK) conjures up frightening images of men in white sheets burning torches. While racism seems to endure in America, the question arises whether the Ku Klux Klan has managed to maintain an interested party of followers. The Unofficial Census looked for some answers.

As we discovered, the Ku Klux Klan currently has 5,000 active members.

While this number represents a significant decrease from the 11,000 who belonged to the Klan in 1981, and the 5 million who belonged in 1925, the number of Americans belonging to other racist groups has swelled to 17,000.

NOTE: Some of the other hate groups active in the United States today include: Identity, a religion followed by 2,000 to 5,000 racists; Neo-Nazis; Posse Comitatus; and Skinheads. The number of hate crimes, the majority of which are not committed by organized groups, has increased dramatically over recent years.

Counting Our Death Row Residents

There is strong popular support for the use of capital punishment. A small group of advocates, however, are pressing the case that the death penalty is racist, and all too often results in great pain and suffering.

There are 2,400 Americans on death rows in 35 of the nation's 38 states that allow capital punishment.

Of the 142 Americans who have been executed since the reinstatement of capital punishment in 1976:

- 79 were white.
- 56 were black.
- 7 were Hispanic.

We also learned that different states employ different methods to carry out their sentences:

METHOD OF EXECUTION	NUMBER KILLED
Electrocution	82
Lethal injection	55
Gas chamber	4
Firing squad	1

NOTE: Two states still authorize the use of firing squads to carry out executions. It is estimated that at least 12 of the last 142 executions have been "botched," indicating that the person remained alive while additional electric shocks or injections were administered.

THE
UNOFFICIAL
U.S.
CENSUS

Counting Atheists

Of America's adults, a vast majority, 170 million, believe in the presence of a God.

Of the country's more than 12 million nonbelievers, half are confirmed atheists. The other 6 million are less certain of their convictions.

NOTE: America's nonbelievers are more likely to be male, better educated, wealthy, and from regions other than the South.

Religion, by Favorable and Unfavorable Perceptions

Since the beginning of recorded history, wars have been fought over religion. Few, if any, subjects elicit a stronger reaction from people. The Unofficial Census counted Americans by their feelings toward some of our religious groups.

As the following table indicates, American adults hold a range of opinions concerning our religious organizations:

RELIGIOUS GROUP	NUMBER VIEWING	
	Favorably	Unfavorably
Protestants	131,328,000	18,240,000
Catholics	131,000,000	23,712,000
Jews	114,912,000	21,888,000
Mormons	76,608,000	56,544,000
Buddhists	45,600,000	60,192,000
Muslims	36,480,000	65,664,000
Jehovah's Witnesses	36,000,000	103,968,000
The New Age Movement	18,240,000	45,600,000
Hare Krishnas	16,416,000	91,200,000

THE
UNOFFICIAL
U.S.
CENSUS

Distribution of U.S. Congress, by Religion

Americans are used to thinking of their politicians in terms of their party affiliation. But politicians have personal lives as well. The Unofficial Census decided to consider the religious leanings of our elected representatives.

As our research indicates, almost all of the country's Congressional representatives maintain religious affiliations. The 535 members of the U.S. Congress belong to the following religious groups:

RELIGION	NUMBER OF CONGRESSMEN
Catholic	142
Methodist	75
Episcopalian	59
Baptist	59
Presbyterian	51
Jewish	41
Protestant	30
Lutheran	22
Mormon	13
United Church of Christ	12
Unitarian	10
Assorted groups	16
Unaffiliated	5

NOTE: The number of Catholic, Jewish, and Mormon members of Congress is at an all-time high. One of the newest religions to gain a member in Congress is the Pan African Orthodox Shrine of the Black Madonna, the faith of Detroit's representative, Barbara Collins.

Prayers—Number Practicing and Frequency

The Unofficial Census counted American adults by their participation in prayer.

As we discovered, virtually every American prays. Looking at this issue further, 137 million Americans pray at least once each week.

Of the faithful, 97 million pray at least once a day, while 42 million pray several times daily.

NOTE: Nearly half of American families, 48 percent, say a prayer or grace before every meal. A larger number, 83 percent, practice the ritual before their holiday meals.

Religious Services, by Number Attending

Nearly two-thirds of American adults belong to a church or synagogue. The Unofficial Census counted Americans by their frequency of attendance at religious services.

As we found, fewer than 1 in 3 American adults, 54 million, attend religious services at least once each week.

On the less devout side of this question, 30 million adults never attend religious services, and an additional 13 million make an appearance less than once each year.

NOTE: Those who frequently attend religious services (more than once a week) are much more likely to be from the South. They are also more likely to be male and less educated.

Believers in Reincarnation

One of life's most thought-provoking questions concerns the issue of reincarnation, the return to life after death as a different physical being. The Unofficial Census counted the number of Americans who believe in reincarnation.

As we discovered, fewer than one-fourth of American adults, 42 million optimists, believe in reincarnation.

NOTE: A larger percentage of teenagers, 31 percent, believe that they will come back, versus only 21 percent of those 50 and older.

Believers in Heaven and Hell

Heaven and hell have always been presented as the reward or punishment for our earthly behaviors. The Unofficial Census counted Americans by their degree of acceptance toward these after-life destinations.

As our research revealed, a large majority of America's adults, 130 million, believe in a heaven.

On the warmer side of this question, a smaller majority of Americans, 98 million adults, believe in the existence of a hell.

Believers in
Angels and Devils

Angels and devils are the symbols of heaven and hell, respectively. The Unofficial Census counted Americans by the number who believe in these supernatural phenomena.

As we learned, half of American adults, 91 million persons, believe in the existence of angels.

Meanwhile, on the naughtier side of this question, a larger number, 100 million Americans, believe in the devil.

Believers in Eternal Life

Most American adults believe in eternal life. These 125 million believers feel that life after death will most likely resemble the following characterizations (in order of those most commonly selected):

1. A union with God
2. A reunion with loved ones
3. A life of peace and tranquility
4. A place of loving intellectual communion
5. A spiritual life
6. A life like the one on earth, only better
7. A paradise of pleasure and delights
8. A life without many of the things which make our present life enjoyable
9. A life of intense action
10. A pale, shadowy form of life

Christmas Behaviors and Practices

More than 192 million Americans celebrate Christmas with a decorated tree. The Unofficial Census tallied the country's participation in a number of other Yuletide rituals.

In addition to enjoying their trees, Americans participate in the following Christmas Day rituals:

CHRISTMAS DAY RITUAL	NUMBER PARTICIPATING
Open presents	130,637,520
Visit family or friends	117,189,540
Attend church	74,924,460
Watch football on TV	59,555,340
Make a fire	28,817,100
Watch a church service on TV	23,053,680
Leave food out for Santa	19,211,400
Go caroling	3,842,280

Americans Choosing Real/Artificial Christmas Trees

As might be expected, a vast majority of Americans, 192,114,000, celebrate Christmas with a tree in their homes. What might not be so obvious are the following statistics from the Unofficial Census:

Nearly half of Americans, 94,135,860, choose to celebrate Christmas with real trees.

A larger number, 97,978,140, choose to use artificial trees for their Christmas celebrations.

A smaller number of Americans, 3,842,280, cannot make up their minds, and use both types.

NOTE: The number of Americans preferring artificial Christmas trees has grown from just 14 percent in 1965 to 51 percent today. Artificial trees are more popular among older Americans, the less affluent, and the less educated. Younger Americans and residents of the Western states still strongly favor the use of real trees.

The Holiday Observances of Jewish Americans

There are an estimated 6,000,000 Jewish persons living in the United States. The Unofficial Census learned the following revealing facts about the holiday behaviors of America's Jews:

✎ Most Jews, 4,740,000, observe Hanukkah with the lighting of candles.

✎ A smaller, but still sizable number of Jews, 1,200,000, have Christmas trees in their homes.

NOTE: Not surprisingly, most of the Jews who observe Christmas are in mixed marriages.

T H E
UNOFFICIAL
U.S.
CENSUS

Distribution of Jewish Religious Observers

The Jewish population is often considered to be very devout in its adherence to religious rituals. The natural question that comes to mind is—how many Jews are very religious, and what specific practices do they follow? The Unofficial Census looked into these spiritual questions.

Our research uncovered the following facts about Jewish Americans:

✎ 480,000 American Jews consider themselves to be Orthodox, the strictest form of Judaism.

✎ A greater number, 1,920,000, consider themselves to be Conservative.

✎ The largest number, 2,040,000, call themselves Reform Jews.

✎ More than one-quarter of the nation's Jews, 1,560,000, are something else (Reconstructionist, etc.).

✎ Additionally, we learned that the following religious rituals are observed by American Jews:

RELIGIOUS RITUAL	NUMBER OF JEWS OBSERVING
Attend Passover Seder	5,400,000
Light Hannukkah candles	4,740,000
Fast on Yom Kippur	3,960,000
Place a mezuzah on the front door	3,780,000
Light Sabbath candles Friday night	2,040,000
Purchase only kosher meat	1,680,000
Keep two sets of dishes for meat and dairy products	1,380,000
Observe the Sabbath in a traditional manner (will not ride, use electricity etc.)	540,000

135

Looking at New Year's Eve Behaviors and Practices

A tremendous amount of pressure is applied on New Year's Eve to stay up late and "party!" The Unofficial Census counted the nation's revelers by their likely New Year's Eve activities. As we learned, this special night tends to be much less exciting than we might expect.

Surprisingly, only 45,600,000 American adults go to a party on New Year's Eve.

The largest number of Americans, 76,608,000, ring in the new year by watching television. An additional 18 million watch a rented movie on their VCRs.

Meanwhile, 41,952,000 "party-poopers" go to sleep before midnight.

New Year's Resolutions, by Number Made and Length of Time Kept

As the Unofficial Census determined, nearly half, 91,200,000, of America's adults commit themselves to New Year's resolutions.

As the following chart illustrates, the number of people who keep their promises decreases significantly with time:

LENGTH OF TIME KEEPING RESOLUTION	NUMBER KEEPING
1 week	70,224,000
1 month	50,160,000
6 months	36,480,000
2 years	17,328,000

NOTE: 70 percent of New Year's resolutions are health-related (stop smoking, lose weight, exercise more, etc.)

The Inclusion of Household Dogs in Holiday Observances

Americans love their dogs. But how many dog-owning Americans include their furry friends in holiday celebrations? The Unofficial Census looked into this canine question.

Our findings indicate that there are more than 41,000,000 dog owners in the United States.

A majority, 28,539,216 dog owners, purchase Christmas presents for their pets.

Also, a surprisingly large number of America's dog owners, 9,843,962, celebrate their dogs' birthdays.

As the following table indicates, Americans celebrate their dogs' birthdays in a variety of ways:

BIRTHDAY CELEBRATION	NUMBER PRACTICING
Give dog a special treat	4,567,598
Make dog a special meal	1,978,636
Give dog a cake	1,850,665
Give dog a new toy	1,801,445
Give dog ice cream	1,102,524
Give dog a new bone	964,708
Sing or wish dog happy birthday	698,921
Give dog a party with other dogs or pets	659,545
Take dog to favorite place	393,758
Take photographs	216,567

NOTE: Not to forget those Americans with "finicky" friends, more than 37 million of America's 57.9 million cats receive Christmas presents from their owners, and more than 13 million have their birthdays celebrated.

The Degree of Adult Closeness to Their Dogs

It has often been said that dogs are "man's best friend." Can this be true or is it just a cute expression? The Unofficial Census decided to find out just how close Americans are to their furry friends.

Interestingly, more than half of American dog owners are more attached to their pets than to at least one other human being. The following profile illustrates how strongly Americans feel about their dogs—and their human counterparts.

Of the country's 41,361,183 dog owners, the following number say that they are as attached to their dogs as to the following persons:

1. Best friend - 13,070,134
2. Children - 6,245,539
3. Spouse - 4,301,563

NOTE: For those who are not yet convinced of America's love of animals, the Unofficial Census learned that 41 percent of America's pet owners display their pet's picture in the home, 8 percent display a picture at work, and 17 percent keep their pet's picture in their wallet or purse.

Preferred Sleeping Locations of America's Dogs

The expression "sleeping like a dog" has become much-used in American language. But what does it say about the sleeping habits of America's dogs? The Unofficial Census decided to determine just where America's dogs do their sleeping.

As our research reveals, America's dogs sleep in a wide variety of locations. Dog owners supplied the following information about where their pets sleep:

Sleeping Location	Number of Dogs Sleeping There
On top of a bed	10,100,000
In a dog house	8,635,500
On the floor	7,524,500
In a dog bed	7,322,500
Outside or in a garage	6,413,500
In their owner's bed	1,262,500

NOTE: A significant majority of America's cats, 67 percent, are allowed to sleep on their owner's bed, or anywhere they want.

Dogs Performing Certain On-Command Tricks

We have all heard of dogs who can fetch the newspaper, get their masters' slippers, or mix a perfect martini—haven't we? But how many of America's dogs actually have talent? The Unofficial Census pondered this creative question.

As our research reveals, slightly more than half of America's dogs, 25,300,500, perform at least one trick. According to America's dog owners, their pets are capable of performing the following tricks on command:

TRICK	NUMBER OF DOGS PERFORMING
Sit	5,313,105
Shake paw	3,795,075
Roll over	2,884,257
Speak	2,681,853
Lie down	1,872,237
Stand on hind legs	1,872,237
Beg	1,821,636
Dance	1,543,331
Sing	759,015
Fetch newspaper	430,109
Say prayers	379,508

Household Dogs and Cats, by Reasons for Owning

With more than 100 million dogs and cats populating American homes, there must be some compelling reason why these pets are acquired in such large numbers. The Unofficial Census counted the reasons behind America's large-scale ownership of cats and dogs.

America's cat and dog owners supplied the following reasons for their having a pet:

REASON FOR OWNING PET	CAT OWNERS	DOG OWNERS
Someone to pet or play with	93%	90%
Companionship	84%	83%
Help children learn responsibility	78%	82%
Someone to communicate with	62%	57%
Security	51%	79%

NOTE: It comes as quite a surprise that more than half of America's cat owners bought their pet for security reasons.

Household Dogs, by Prevalence of Obesity

It turns out that many of "man's best friends" are also man's fattest friends. At latest count, approximately 20,200,000 of America's 50,500,000 dogs are overweight.

The Prevalence of Old Age in Household Dogs—Centenarians

Veterinary science has calculated that the average year of a dog's life is roughly equivalent to 7 human years. So just how aged are America's dogs and how many have lived past the elusive 100-year mark? The Unofficial Census looked into these timely questions.

Our research indicates that America's 50.5 million dogs have an average age of 6 years and, as the following table reveals, have ages over the following distribution:

AGE OF DOG	NUMBER INCLUDED
Less than 1 year	2,474,500
5 years or less	24,745,000
Between 5 and 10 years	16,867,000
Between 10 and 15 years	6,514,500
Older than 15 years	1,161,500

NOTE: According to our calculations, roughly 10,857,500 American dogs have achieved senior citizen status, and 2,676,500 have become centenarians (100 years old or older).

Counting U.S. Bird Cages and Their Occupants

While Americans own cats and dogs in large numbers, more than 50 million of each pet, Americans keep other pets as well. Bird ownership, for example, has increased more than 10 percent over the past five years. The Unofficial Census decided to look into this flighty issue in greater detail.

As our research reveals, there are 12,895,000 pet birds living in 5.2 million American homes.

While the majority of pet bird households, 3.3 million, own 1 bird, 520,000 homes own 4 or more birds.

N O T E : Strangely, nearly half of bird-owning homes, 2.4 million, also own a cat, a traditional predator to birds. ''Better keep the gate shut, Tweetie.''

Household Pets— Rodents, Etc.

While Americans pamper many pets that would be considered major sources of food in many less developed countries, they also harbor certain pets that many consider to be disgusting. The Unofficial Census looked into this strange subject.

As our research reveals, Americans do indeed own a large number of "strange pets":

Pet Type	Number of Americans Owning
Rabbits	1,540,978
Hamsters	1,021,130
Guinea pigs	501,282
Goats, sheep, etc.	408,452
Pigeons, ducks, etc.	445,584
Rats, mice, etc.	380,603
Gerbils	371,320
Turtles	324,905
Ferrets	194,943
Lizards	120,679
Snakes	102,113

Counting America's Research Animals

The use of animals in laboratory research has become a practice shrouded in controversy. The business and research communities defend the practice as necessary to their search for new products, drugs, and vaccines, while protesters cite the tremendous pain endured by innocent animals. The Unofficial Census looked into this timely issue.

Our research indicates that at least 70 million animals are used (and die) in research each year. Included in this number are the following animals:

Animal Used in Laboratory Research	Number Used
Mice	45,000,000
Rats	15,000,000
Birds	5,000,000
Frogs	3,000,000
Hamsters	1,000,000
Guinea Pigs	1,000,000
Rabbits	750,000
Dogs	250,000
Ungulates (horses, cattle, etc.)	200,000
Cats	100,000
Primates (monkeys, etc.)	25,000

NOTE: While the number of animals used in research has reportedly dropped by more than 50 percent since 1968, animal rights groups estimate that today's number is closer to 100 million used each year, due to nonreporting by private sector researchers.

147

Phobics, by Sources of Fear

Almost everyone is afraid of something. According to our research, the following things elicit fear in the greatest number of Americans:

Scary Thing	Number Afraid of This
Snakes	100,983,000
Public speaking	64,038,000
High spaces	46,797,000
Mice	39,408,000
Flying on a plane	39,400,000
Spiders and insects	27,093,000

Musophobics, by Gender

Musophobia is the fear of mice. But how many people could possibly consider such a small animal a serious threat, and is it true that women are more afraid of mice? The Unofficial Census set out in search of some answers to these tiny questions.

As our research reveals, nearly half of America's adults, 83,452,511 persons, view mice as the most feared household pest.

And, as the stereotype correctly alleges, a majority of musophics are women:

GENDER	NUMBER MUSOPHICS
Men	31,152,481
Women	52,300,030

Dental Phobics

Visiting the dentist is certainly one of the more unpleasant experiences known to humankind. It is beyond the financial reach of many Americans. As a result, a large number of Americans have never visited the dentist.

The Unofficial Census learned that 11,565,000 Americans have never visited a dentist.

As the following chart reveals, a disproportionately large number of these Americans live in the South:

Region	Number Never Visiting A Dentist	%
Northeast	1,639,000	3.8
Midwest	2,205,000	3.9
South	5,235,000	6.5
West	2,486,000	5.1

NOTE: In addition to residents of the South, black Americans are also less likely to have ever received dental care. On a more positive note, the number of Americans who have never known the pleasures, and resulting dental health, of the dentist's chair has decreased in recent years.

Counting Employed Americans and Their Teeth

An estimated 40 million Americans have avoided a visit to the dentist because of fear. In light of this fact, the Unofficial Census decided to consider the state of America's teeth.

Our research results indicate the following information about the teeth of America's 116,657,944 workers:

Fewer than half, 42,762,121 workers, have all 28 of their teeth.

A significant number, 4,911,611, have no teeth at all.

The following table provides a complete count of teeth in American workers:

Number of Teeth	Number of Workers Having
0	4,911,611
1	58,333
Between 2 and 5	734,992
Between 6 and 10	4,118,286
Between 11 and 20	10,394,881
Between 21 and 27	53,677,720
All 28	42,762,121

Counting Employed Americans and Their Cavities

The Unofficial Census learned the following insights about America's 116,657,944 workers:

   A small minority, 4,666,318, have no cavities.

   A majority, 59,145,578, have more than 18 cavities.

   A larger minority, 21,465,062, have more than 40 cavities.

NOTE: The average American worker has 23 cavities. Our findings also reveal that female workers tend to have more cavities than their male counterparts.

Braces—Number
of Adults Wearing

For many kids, orthodonture is an unavoidable, and necessary, evil. For an increasing number of adults, however, braces represent an effective way to improve their appearance.

Of America's adults, 1,215,000 have braces on their teeth. Of these, 300,000 are men.

U.S. Denture Clusters

Fascinated by the number of denture adhesive commercials on television, the Unofficial Census decided that a closer look at this dental phenomenon was absolutely necessary.

Our research findings indicate that a large number of Americans, 51,723,000 persons, wear dentures.

Surprisingly, 2,480,302 of these toothless individuals are under the age of 30.

Not surprisingly, the proportion of denture wearers increases with age, with more than half of those 60 and older wearing false teeth.

Disposal Diaper Use in America, by Age of Wearer

A growing number of Americans are wearing diapers. This growth, however, is not entirely due to an increase in the nation's birthrate.

The Unofficial Census learned that more than 20.5 million Americans wear diapers.

Of these individuals, only 9.5 million are children.

The remaining 11 million diaper wearers are adults suffering from urinary incontinence.

NOTE: Of the 11 million adults who suffer from incontinence, approximately 90 percent can be treated or cured. Few of these sufferers, however, have sought professional help.

Health Remedies, by Use of Illegal or Unproven Products

It often takes many years for new drugs and vaccines to pass through the necessary procedures for federal licensing. Many Americans, however, desperate for relief, find hope in health products that are only available in other countries or through domestic black-market sources.

More than one-fourth of American adults, 47,424,000, have turned to health remedies that are not yet licensed for use in the United States.

Not surprisingly, a large number of these desperate Americans are suffering from painful, debilitating diseases.

For example, more than 11 million of America's 31 million arthritis sufferers have used unproven drugs.

Also, nearly 1 million of today's 6 million living cancer patients have experimented with illegal remedies.

Steroid Use—
Incidence in Children

There has been a great deal of attention focused recently on the illegal use of black-market anabolic-androgenic steroids (AAS) by professional and amateur athletes. The Unofficial Census decided to determine the extent to which synthetic steroids are being abused.

Our research indicates that an estimated 1 million Americans take AAS for nonmedical reasons.

Additional findings include the fact that, of the 6,700,000 boys in American high schools, more than 6 percent, 402,000, are using steroids to build muscles or "improve their appearance."

Astonishingly, more than two-thirds of these child users, 268,000 children, started using steroids at age 15 or younger.

NOTE: It is estimated that Americans spend between $300 million and $500 million for black-market steroids each year. This is an increase from $100 million just last year, and a disturbing indicator of America's growing use of steroids.

Human Organs— Distribution by Number Waiting for Transplants

With recent advances in medical science have come the opportunity for many Americans to receive life-sustaining organ transplants. A problem may develop, however, when the demand for certain organs is greater than the supply. The Unofficial Census counted the number of Americans who are waiting for their "special delivery."

At the present time, more than 21,000 Americans are on waiting lists to receive organ transplants. Of these, the following number are waiting for certain types of organs:

ORGAN	NUMBER WAITING FOR ONE
Kidney	17,940
Heart	1,763
Liver	1,216
Pancreas	472
Lung	308

NOTE: Many Americans have expressed concerns about the preponderance of organ recipients who are young, white, and wealthy. As evidence of an imbalanced system, the average black kidney recipient waits 13.9 months for his organ, while a white recipient waits just 7.6 months.

THE
UNOFFICIAL
U.S.
CENSUS

Counting America's Brain-Dead

The "right to die" has become an explosive issue in recent years. With religious advocates on one side, and concerned relatives on the other, the helpless patient often lies in the middle. The Unofficial Census looked into this issue in greater detail.

As we discovered, there are approximately 15,000 Americans in a persistent vegetative state (PVS). These individuals have no cognitive function and, according to the current laws of 28 states, must be kept alive by all possible means.

At the present time, only one-third of American adults, 60 million, have wills. An even smaller number, 27 million, have living wills—legal provisions which allow an individual to decide whether he or she can be kept alive on life support systems.

NOTE: Relatives are currently allowed to discontinue a person's life support in 22 states. Life support is ceased, though informally, in many other states as well.

Looking at Frozen Americans

A great deal of attention, and humor, has been focused on the use of "cryonic suspension." In this process, humans are frozen after their deaths in the hope that they can be brought back to life when a cure for their fatal disease has been discovered.

At latest count, 25 Americans are in the state of "cryonic suspension."

Another 300 Americans have paid in advance to receive cryonic services upon their deaths.

NOTE: We are told that, contrary to popular speculation, Walt Disney is not one of the 25 Americans "on ice."

Personal Ambitions—
Distribution by
Those Achieved

Every American has certain goals and aspirations for the future. Some have achieved at least a few of their dreams. The Unofficial Census counted America's adults by their dreams and their achievements:

CONDITION	NUMBER DREAMING OF	NUMBER HAVING
Home ownership	156,864,000	109,440,000
Happy marriage	140,448,000	100,320,000
Owning a car	131,328,000	149,568,000
Having children	131,000,000	113,088,000
Being rich	113,000,000	7,296,000
Interesting job	111,264,000	60,192,000

Preferred Home Activities of American Adults

According to our research findings, American adults have clear preferences when it comes to their time at home. As the following chart illustrates, America's top home activities are:

HOME ACTIVITY	NUMBER PREFERRING
Spending time with family	142,272,000
Making love	114,912,000
Listening to music	105,792,000
Reading	83,904,000
Beautifying home	80,256,000
Cooking	63,840,000
Entertaining	60,192,000
Home improvement	56,544,000
Watching television	54,720,000
Pampering self	52,896,000

NOTE: Not surprisingly, when taken separately, a majority of men name "making love" as their top choice. The greatest number of women say that spending time with their family gives them the greatest joy.

Romantics—
Distribution by
Gender and Region

A majority of American adults, 143 million, claim to be "romantic."

While 80 percent of men say they fall into this category, nearly as many women, 77 percent, claim this distinction.

Residents of the Northeast are most likely to be romantic. The Midwest, on the other hand, has the lowest percentage of amorous individuals.

Americans Using Certain Terms of Endearment

Most Americans have a special name for their "certain somebody." In fact, only 6 percent of American adults simply use their partner's first name when addressing that person. The Unofficial Census answered that pressing question—what is the country's most popular pet name?

In what will likely come as a surprise to many, the term "honey" is by far the most popular term of endearment, favored by more than 26 percent of American adults.

With 47,803,392 persons in this country being called "honey," the following chart answers our natural next question—what are the country's other most popular pet names?

1 Honey
2 Baby
3 Sweetheart
4 Dear
5 Lover
6 Darling
7 Sugar
8 Pumpkin
9 Angel*
10 Precious
11 Beautiful*

*Indicates a tie with the previous entry.

The following chart places the country's "honeys" by geographic region:

Region	Number of Adults Called "Honey"	%
Northeast	11,506,704	31
Midwest	13,627,104	31
South	13,964,544	22
West	8,705,040	23

Incidence of Staying-Up Late, Distribution by Activity

America has a surprisingly large number of "night owls." Of America's 182 million adults, 67,488,000 stay up past midnight on any given evening. These "late-nighters" cited the following reasons for their nocturnal behavior:

LATE-NIGHT ACTIVITY	NUMBER PARTICIPATING
Watched television	41,842,560
Read	21,596,160
Ate a snack	14,847,360
Listened to radio	12,822,720
Did housework	9,448,320
Worked late	9,448,320
Made a phone call	7,423,680

NOTE: Burning the midnight oil is more pervasive among young Americans. 51 percent of Americans age 18 to 29 stay up past midnight on any given evening, while only 22 percent of those age 60 or older do so.

Insomniacs and Methods Used to Fall Asleep

While everyone has trouble getting to sleep at some time in their lives, a large number of American adults, 29,913,600 persons, suffer from serious insomnia.

We also learned that all Americans use the following methods to help them get to sleep:

METHOD	NUMBER USING
Watch television	60,192,000
Read	54,720,000
Exercise	23,712,000
Meditation	23,712,000
Medication	16,416,000

NOTE: While it is not clear whether sleep disturbances are the cause or the result of psychiatric disorders, those individuals with sleep disorders are nearly three times more likely to also suffer from psychiatric problems.

Counting America's Sleepers, by Type of Sleepwear

The Unofficial Census considered the types of sleepwear preferred by American adults.

As the following table illustrates, America's adults have a wide range of preferences when it comes to their use (or nonuse) of certain types of sleepwear:

TYPE OF SLEEPWEAR	NUMBER SLEEPING IN	
	MEN	WOMEN
Pajamas	32,932,623	17,744,653
Underwear	29,372,339	3,735,716
Nude	16,911,347	5,603,575
"Long johns"	1,780,142	933,929
Nighties/nightgowns	—	58,837,534

Dreamers—
Distribution
by Age, etc.

Dreams have been the subject of many serious psychological theories. The Unofficial Census looked into the nature of dreaming in today's American adults.

As we discovered, a majority of American adults, 124 million, usually dream while sleeping.

Of these dreamers, the greatest number, 50 million, say they usually dream in color. A smaller number, 29 million, report that they most often dream in black and white. The remaining number split their time between the two.

Additionally, a majority of dreamers, 81 million, remember their dreams as including sound. Just 24 million remember them as being silent. The remaining number remember a mix of the two.

NOTE: Americans are less likely to dream as they get older. Women are also more likely to dream than their male counterparts.

Snoring—Prevalence

Snoring has long been the object of humorous attention. Recently, however, the scientific community has turned its attention toward this disturbing problem. The Unofficial Census decided to do the same.

As we discovered, a majority of American adults, 111,811,200, are snorers.

Of these "wood-sawers," 24,806,400 snore loudly enough to be disturbing to their spouses.

NOTE: Some recent estimates put the number of problem snorers at as many as 60 million Americans. Snoring tends to occur more frequently in men and older persons.

Morning Rituals in American Homes

Mornings mean different things to different Americans. In an effort to find out what Americans do with their morning time, the Unofficial Census turned its sights toward this issue.

According to our findings, Americans find certain activities indispensable to their morning routines. The following activities were named by America's 182,400,000 adults as part of their *every* morning:

ACTIVITY	NUMBER DOING EVERY MORNING
Personal hygiene	153,216,000
Listen to the radio	100,320,000
Drink coffee	96,672,000
Make the bed	96,672,000
Eat breakfast	91,200,000
Kiss spouse/partner	89,376,000
Read the newspaper	63,840,000
Watch television	54,720,000
Exercise	40,128,000
Iron clothes	20,064,000
Make love	12,768,000

Shower Duration Characteristics of American Adults

It always seems like the other person in the house uses all of the hot water when they take a shower. But do Americans really take long showers, or does it just feel that way? The Unofficial Census took the plunge in search of some answers.

Our research indicates that American adults take showers of the following duration:

SHOWER DURATION	NUMBER TAKING
1 minute or less	364,800
5 minutes or less	41,222,400
Less than 10 minutes	133,881,600
Between 10 and 15 minutes	40,492,800
More than 15 minutes	5,836,800
20 minutes or more	1,094,400

Flossers

We have all been told of the importance of flossing. But how many Americans follow this healthy advice? This question was a natural for the Unofficial Census.

As we discovered, just over half of the nation's adult population makes flossing a part of their hygienic lives. An estimated 96,124,800 American adults report using dental floss regularly.

NOTE: The average flosser uses nearly 11 yards of floss each month, more than 5 miles of floss over the course of an average lifetime.

Coffee Consumption Habits in American Adults

As most of us already know, Americans love coffee. The Unofficial Census decided to turn its attention to the issue of coffee consumption in America.

As we discovered, a majority of American adults, 113,088,000 drink coffee. What we also found, however, is a wide variation in the number of "cups of mud" Americans consume each day.

Daily Cups of Coffee	Number Consuming
1 cup	31,008,000
2 cups	27,360,000
3 cups	18,240,000
4 cups	12,768,000
5 or more cups	21,888,000

Kosher Food Consumers, by Religion

$\mathbf{A}$ large and growing number of Americans, 6,000,000, routinely eat Kosher foods.

Interestingly, just over one quarter of these individuals, 1,800,000 are Jewish.

NOTE: The number of kosher products on the market has grown to 17,000 today, from just 1,000 in 1978. This dramatic growth is attributed to the increased religious observance of many young Jews and the growth in demand by non-Jews and other religions that believe that kosher food is cleaner and of higher quality. Other religions that require diets similar to those of Orthodox Jews include Seventh-day Adventists and Muslims.

Snake, Eel, Sushi, Etc.—Number Eating

America has traditionally been known as a country of "meat and potatoes" eaters. More exotic foods have remained the domain of Europeans and other sophisticates. Intrigued by this stereotype, the Unofficial Census set out to count the number of Americans who have broken out of this mold and sampled exotic foods. Our findings reveal some interesting facts about America's willingness to sample unusual foods.

As the following table illustrates, many Americans are willing to try new foods:

Food	Number Who Have Tried
Venison	98,496,900
Snails	36,480,000
Tofu	36,480,000
Sushi	34,656,000
Steak tartare	32,832,000
Eel	20,064,000
Snake	14,592,000

NOTE: Surprisingly, younger Americans (ages 18 to 29) are least likely to sample most of these unusual foods.

T H E
UNOFFICIAL
U.S.
CENSUS

Looking at Caviar Fanciers

Our findings indicate that 54,745,500 Americans have tried caviar.

Interestingly, of those who have tried it, only 4,379,640 really like it.

Snackers—Their Munchies By Timing and Frequency

Snacking is an American obsession. Americans spend more than $10 billion each year on snack food. And while more than a third of Americans say they would like to cut down on their snacking, 86 percent of American adults, 156,864,000 persons, continue to snack between meals.

The Unofficial Census obtained the following insights about snackers—when they prefer to snack and what they most like to consume.

As the following table indicates, snackers practice their art at many different times of the day. In addition to the 21,960,960 Americans who snack all day long, certain specific times were most popular among our nation's munchers:

PREFERRED SNACKING TIME	NUMBER SNACKING
Before lunch	10,980,480
Afternoons	29,804,160
Before dinner	15,686,400
After dinner	26,666,880
Before bed	25,098,240

NOTE: Interestingly, more than half of our nation's snackers, 98,824,320, snack at least twice each day and a significant number, 3,137,280, consume 10 or more snacks daily.

Snackers, by Incidence of "Snackers' Remorse"

As might be expected, a number of people who treat themselves to unhealthy between-meal snacks are visited by feelings of guilt. But how many Americans suffer from "snackers' remorse"? The Unofficial Census, always intrigued by such issues, looked into this matter.

Approximately one in three snackers, 52,235,712 Americans, feel guilty about their habit. What is more surprising, however, is the degree to which these individuals feel guilty for their actions. Many snackers consider their actions to be on a par with certain significant ethical violations.

The following table illustrates the number of American adults who feel greater guilt about their snacking than these ethical lapses:

Issue	Number Feeling Greater Guilt About Snacking
Lying about weight	28,235,520
Lying about age	25,098,240
Lying to a friend	18,823,680
Breaking a date	17,255,040
Cheating on taxes	17,255,040
Taking a phony sick day	15,686,400

U.S. Heartburn
Sufferers

All of us have been bothered by heartburn at some time in our lives. But how many Americans suffer from serious heartburn, and what are these unfortunate individuals doing to deal with this painful malady? In response to these pressing questions, the Unofficial Census set out to find some relief, and some answers.

Our findings indicate that 80,256,000 Americans suffer from regular (at least once within the past month) heartburn. Of these, 22,800,000 are more frequent sufferers, experiencing major symptoms more than twice each week.

The following table illustrates some of the most common causes of heartburn, as cited by these chronic sufferers:

Cause of Heartburn	Number Citing
Spicy foods	20,748,000
Stress	14,592,000
Family arguments	10,944,000
Overexcitement	9,348,000
Depression	8,208,000

U.S. Constipation Clusters

Judging by the number of laxative commercials presented on television, we can only assume that there are a large number of constipated Americans. In an effort to find out just how many of our fellow countrymen and -women are plagued by this twelve-letter condition, the Unofficial Census took a demographic look at constipation.

As our suspicions bear out, there are 25,980,928 Americans aged 12 or older who suffer from constipation. Of those, 7,104,160 are men and 18,876,768 are women.

The following chart demonstrates the geographic distribution of America's constipated residents:

Region	Number Constipated	%
Northeast	5,637,861	13.2
Midwest	6,183,462	14.4
South	7,794,278	18.2
West	6,365,327	14.8

NOTE: There is a greater likelihood that residents of Southern states will be constipated. In addition, blacks, women, older Americans, the less active, the less affluent, and the less educated are also more likely to suffer. Given the prevalence of this ailment, it comes as no surprise that over $330 million is spent on over-the-counter laxatives each year.

The Incidence of Flatulence in Americans

Our research into this disturbing subject area revealed the following results:

An estimated 30 million Americans (and their neighbors) are plagued by chronic excess intestinal gas (flatulence).

Unfortunately, it is reported that very few of these afflicted Americans have sought medical assistance.

The Incidence of Too Heavy, Too Skinny, and Just Right Americans

Our research reveals the following information about the state of America's weight:

More than one-quarter, 51,911,040, of American adults are overweight.

A significant number, 13,169,280, are underweight.

A majority of American adults, 117,319,680, weigh within the normal range.

Dieters—Their
Numbers and Methods

Our research indicates that nearly one in four American adults, 48 million persons, is on a diet at any given time. While this number represents a substantial decline from the nearly 65 million Americans who were dieting in 1986, the market for diet products has grown to more than $33 billion.

Dieters use a wide variety of means to achieve their goals:

DIETING TECHNIQUE	NUMBER PRACTICING
Cut down on high-calorie foods	46,560,000
Exercise	42,240,000
Use low-fat foods and beverages	41,280,000
Use low-calorie foods and beverages	39,360,000
Count calories	20,640,000
Skip meals	13,920,000
Attend weight-loss classes	8,160,000
Crash diet	5,760,000
Use diet meal substitutes	5,280,000
Use diet pills	1,920,000

NOTE: Between 75 and 90 percent of dieters who lose weight later regain it. Consequently, it is not surprisingly to learn that the average dieter makes 3 attempts to lose weight each year.

THE
UNOFFICIAL
U.S.
CENSUS

Diet Food Consumption, by Dieters and Non-Dieters

Americans spend nearly $15 billion each year on diet foods. As the Unofficial Census discovered, these products are being consumed by more than just dieters.

While an estimated 48 million Americans are on diets, a majority of American adults, 93 million persons, consume low-calorie foods and beverages.

And, while the number of dieters has contracted by 17 million since 1986, the number of Americans consuming diet food products has grown by 15 million persons.

The most popular *diet foods* consumed by Americans include the following products:

DIET FOOD PRODUCT	NUMBER CONSUMING
Beverages	65,100,000
Dairy products	60,450,000
Frozen desserts	42,780,000
Baked goods	37,200,000
Snack foods	35,340,000
Dinners	29,760,000

Counting Couch Potatoes

Much attention has been paid recently to America's leanings toward inactivity, poor diet, and addiction to television. But how many Americans truly classify as "couch potatoes"? A few, a peck, a bushel? The Unofficial Census looked into this question.

Our research indicates that there are indeed a large number of "potatoes" populating our country's couches. According to our findings, there are an estimated 106 million American adults who are sedentary (the technical term for C.P.s). To qualify as a sedentary adult, a person must exercise less than 20 minutes three times each week.

Our nation's "couch potatoes" blame certain factors for their inactivity. The following reasons were given for not being more active:

REASON FOR BEING A COUCH POTATO	NUMBER CITING
Not enough time	60,420,000
Not enough self-discipline	54,060,000
No interesting activity available	48,760,000
No partner available	47,000,000
Not enough money	46,640,000

THE UNOFFICIAL U.S. CENSUS

Counting Baby Couch Potatoes

Our research findings indicate that sedentary behavior is not limited to American adults.

An estimated 20 percent of American children, 12,780,000 kids, are obese.

NOTE: At least 29 states do not require their schools to provide more than 10 minutes of physical education each day.

Television Viewing Patterns—Non-Users and Heavy Users

With televisions occupying a place of honor in nearly every American home, the question that comes to mind is—how many Americans are "addicted" to the century's most influential invention? The Unofficial Census looked into this question.

As our research indicates, a number of American adults, 6,007,186 persons, rarely or never watch television. The remaining majority of Americans, however, watch a great deal of television, more than four hours daily on average. The following table illustrates the variations in America's TV viewing habits:

Hours of TV Watched Daily	Number Watching
1 hour or less	33,312,575
Between 1 and 5 hours	124,330,539
More than 5 hours	18,567,664
More than 10 hours	3,458,682
More than 15 hours	1,274,251

Television Viewers, by Type of Programs Regularly Watched

Of America's adults, a large majority, 176,392,814 watch TV frequently. The Unofficial Census counted these individuals by the types of programs they most commonly view.

As the following table illustrates, America's television viewers have strong preferences when it comes to the programs they watch:

Type of Television Program	Number Watching Regularly
Movies	111,127,473
News/documentaries	91,724,263
Situation comedies	79,376,766
Sports	70,557,126
Police/detective stories	63,501,413

Television Viewers, by Number of Programs Watched at the Same Time

Since the introduction of the television remote control, it has become easier for today's viewers to change the channel. The Unofficial Census decided to assess the degree to which Americans are making use of this influential new technology.

As our numbers reveal, Americans are changing the channel more often.

While a majority of adult viewers, 91,200,000, still choose to stay with a single program, a large number prefer to scan the dial.

Nearly one-fourth of adult viewers, 69,312,000 Americans, follow 2 or more television programs simultaneously.

Of these fickle viewers, more than half, 23,712,000, follow 3 or more programs at the same time.

NOTE: With 75 percent of American homes now armed with a remote control for their television, it is easier for today's couch potatoes to scan the dial.

190

Television Channel Changers— Distribution by Motivation

A large number of Americans choose to watch more than one television program at the same time. The Unofficial Census decided to investigate the reasons behind this capricious behavior.

As our research revealed, the nation's 69,312,000 multi-program viewers attribute their ''itchy fingers'' to the following causes:

Cause of Multi-Program Viewing	Number Giving This Reason
To see what else is on	19,407,360
Get bored with program	18,021,120
To avoid commercials	13,169,280
To monitor several shows	9,010,560

Television Commercials, by Viewer Perception

Television advertising has always drawn a strong reaction from viewers. While 20 percent of today's viewers say that they enjoy watching television commercials, 14 percent find them distasteful enough to leave the room when they are on, and 11 percent feel sufficiently motivated by their presence to change the channel.

Our research indicates that American adults hold a generally negative view toward today's TV ads:

IMAGE OF TV ADS	NUMBER AGREEING
Misleading	60,192,000
Insulting	58,368,000
Boring	58,368,000
Informative	38,304,000
Entertaining	34,656,000

VCR Owners, by Their Ability to Program Their Machines

A majority of Americans, 179,520,000, live in homes with VCRs.

Of those, a surprisingly large number, 143,616,000, are unable to program their VCRs to record television shows off-the-air.

VCR Owners— Distribution by Type of Videos Rented

More than 122 million Americans own VCRs. And while very few of these Americans are able to program their machines to record, most, if not all, are able to play a prerecorded tape. The Unofficial Census counted today's VCR owners by the inclination to rent certain types of videocassettes.

As the following table illustrates, VCR owners have strong preferences when it comes to their video renting choices:

VIDEO GENRE	NUMBER RENTING
Comedies	78,080,000
Action and adventure	63,440,000
Dramas	50,020,000
Children's movies and cartoons	26,840,000
Music videos	13,420,000
Sports	10,980,000
Adult movies	7,320,000
Exercise	3,660,000

NOTE: As we might expect, men are more likely to rent the following types of videos: action and adventure, sports, and adult movies. Also coming as no surprise is the finding that women are more likely to rent dramas, children's movies, and cartoons.

Phones, by Frequency of Listed and Unlisted Numbers

The Unofficial Census counted the number of Americans with phone service. As we discovered, almost all Americans, 229,059,000, have phones.

A significant number of these Americans, 13,743,540, live in homes with two or more phone numbers.

Interestingly, nearly half of the Americans who have phone service, 89,330,100 persons, have chosen to have unlisted phone numbers.

NOTE: Unlisted numbers are more likely to belong to younger and single Americans. Perhaps as a result of the recent surge in telemarketing, the number of Americans with unlisted phone numbers has increased dramatically in recent years.

Counting Our Phones

As the price of telephones drops, more and more Americans are placing units throughout their homes. The Unofficial Census counted Americans by the number of phones in their homes.

As the following table illustrates, a large number of Americans live in multi-phone homes:

NUMBER OF PHONES IN HOME	NUMBER LIVING IN THESE HOMES
1	61,845,930
2	80,170,650
3	50,392,980
4	22,905,900
5 or more	13,743,540

NOTE: Regardless of the number of phones a person may buy, it still always seems to be ringing in the other room.

196

Radio Listeners, Favorite Formats

The average American listens to radio almost 3 hours each day. In view of this considerable commitment, the Unofficial Census counted Americans by their favorite radio formats.

As the following chart reveals, American adults can be separated by their preferences for certain radio formats:

RADIO FORMAT	NUMBER LISTENING
Adult contemporary	35,568,000
Contemporary hits	33,379,200
Country	26,083,200
Album-oriented rock	19,699,200
Easy listening	14,774,400
Oldies	14,409,600
Urban contemporary	13,680,000
News/talk	5,836,800

Counting Our Radios, by Household Location

Americans own 343 million radios. That comes to nearly 5.6 radios per home. The Unofficial Census counted our nation's radios by their household location:

Location	Number of Radios Placed There
Bedrooms	172,300,000
Living rooms	63,300,000
Kitchens	46,200,000
Bathrooms	14,700,000
Dining rooms	13,300,000

NOTE: Americans also have 131 million radios in their cars, and 38 million in their trucks, vans, and RVs.

Moviegoers—
Distribution by
Frequency of
Attendance

Americans love going to the movies. Driven by the fact that more than 1 billion movie admissions are recorded each year, the Unofficial Census decided to explore the issue of moviegoing in American adults.

Of this nation's adults, 113,088,000 attend at least one movie each year. Of these moviegoers, 41 million attend movies frequently (at least once a month).

On the other side of this question, a large number of adults, 63,840,000, claim to never go to movies.

NOTE: America's most frequent moviegoers are more likely to be from the West or Northeast, wealthier, better educated, and younger.

Teenage Moviegoers— Distribution by Frequency of Attendance

The Unofficial Census counted America's teenagers by their attendance at motion pictures.

As we discovered, a large majority of America's 20,522,000 teenagers (ages 12 to 17), nearly 20 million kids, go to movies. Of these moviegoing kids, nearly half, 9 million, attend movies frequently (at least once a month).

On the less socially active side of this question, fewer than 500,000 teenagers claim to never go to movies.

Moviegoers—
Distribution by
Favorite Genres

More than 113 million American adults go to movies. The Unofficial Census counted these movie aficionados by their favorite movie genres.

Comedies are the current film favorites of 20 million adults, followed closely by action adventures, favored by 18 million; dramas, 12 million; science fiction, 5 million; romance, 3 million; and musicals, 2 million.

Movie Content—
Adult Attitudes
Toward

It seems like there is always at least one organized group complaining about the amount of sex, violence, or profanity in today's motion pictures. The Unofficial Census counted America's adults by their attitudes concerning today's movies.

At latest count, a large majority of adults feel there is either too much violence, profanity, or nudity in most of today's movies.

The largest number, 150 million, believe there is too much violence.

The second loudest complaint, voiced by 146 million, is against too much profanity.

The third, and weakest, complaint comes against nudity. Just over 131 million adults say there is too much nudity in today's movies.

NOTE: The largest number of complainers tend to be female, older, less educated, less wealthy, black or Hispanic, conservative, and hail from Southern states.

Movie Attitudes, by Impact on Attendance

At latest count, a large majority of American adults are concerned about the amount of violence, profanity, and nudity in today's movies. The Unofficial Census decided to see what, if any, impact this concern has on the frequency of movie attendance.

At latest count, a majority of adults say that they would be less likely to see a movie that contains either violence, profanity, or nudity.

The largest number of those who fall into this category, 109 million, are less likely to see a movie that contains violence. Meanwhile, 5 million adults say they are more likely to see a violent picture.

The second largest group, containing 104 million adults, say they are less likely to see a movie which contains profanity. Fewer than 4 million adults are more likely to attend a movie with bad language.

Also repelling nearly 104 million adults are movies that feature nudity. In contrast to their profane relatives, however, more than 7 million adults would be more likely to see a movie if it included nudity.

NOTE: True to their feelings about violence, profanity, and nudity in movies, likely boycotters are more likely to be older, less educated, conservative, less wealthy, female, and hail from a Southern state.

Counting the Stars— on Hollywood Boulevard

One of the greatest honors in show business is to receive a star on Hollywood Boulevard. The Unofficial Census couldn't resist the urge to investigate this show biz phenomenon.

At latest count, there are 1,927 show business luminaries who have been honored with stars on Hollywood Boulevard.

Of these lucky figures, 2 are animals (Rin Tin Tin and Lassie).

NOTE: With only 2,518 available spaces, just 591 more stars can be added to Hollywood's Walk of Fame.

Satisfaction With Life—Distribution

The Unofficial Census looked at the quality of life among today's adults.

As we learned, a large majority of Americans, 162 million adults, report being satisfied with their lives. Of these "happy Americans," more than 82 million are "very satisfied" with their lives.

What's more, nearly 104 million Americans are happier today than they were 5 years ago.

NOTE: Not surprisingly, "satisfied Americans" tend to be wealthier, better educated, and white.

Sources

PAGE

1. National Center for Health Statistics
2. American Fertility Society Center for Surrogate Parenting (cited in *USA Today*)
3. National Opinion Research Center (NORC)
4. NORC
5. Dr. Stephen Kaplan
6. Same
7. R.H. Bruskin Associates
8. NORC
9. NORC
10. NORC
11. National Guild of Hypnotists
12. Gallup (cited in Research Alert)
    Dr. Stephen Kaplan
13. Dr. Stephen Kaplan
14. Gallup (cited in Research Alert)
    Dr. Stephen Kaplan
15. The Vampire Institute
16. *The New York Times*
17. American Association of Blood Banks (cited in *USA Today*)
18. The Naturist Society
19. The Naturist Society
    USA Today

20. *Journal of the American Medical Association (JAMA)*
    In Health
21. American Music Conference
22. *Psychology Today*
23. American Music Conference
    The New York Times
24. American Philatelic Society
25. American Numismatic Association
26. *The Encyclopedia of Associations*
    Ship in Bottle Association
27. Hobby Industries of America
28. Faber-Castell
29. National Horseshoe Pitchers Association
30. *American Demographics*
31. Center for the Study of Sport in Society
32. National Golf Foundation (cited in *USA Today*)
33. National Basketball Association (cited in *USA Today*)
34. *The New York Times*
35. *Forbes* (cited in *USA Today*)
36. *JAMA*
37. *JAMA*
38. *JAMA*
39. *JAMA*
40. *The New York Times*
    JAMA

41. *JAMA*
42. *Newsweek*
   The New York Times
43. *American Demographics*
   The New York Times
   American Health
44. NORC
45. "How Big is Big" (cited in
   Cosmopolitan)
46. Dr. Richard Sipe
47. Korbel Champagne Cellars
48. *Psychology Today*
49. NORC
50. NORC
51. National Center for Health
   Statistics
   American Journal of Public Health
   Newsweek
52. *Newsweek*
   American Journal of Public Health
   Zero Population Growth
53. Alan Guttmacher Institute
54. Bureau of Labor Statistics
   USA Today
55. Lenore/Rhyne College,
   Department of Education
56. Home School Legal Defense
   Association
   The New York Times
57. NORC
58. Bicycle Institute of America
   University of California,
   Berkeley (Wellness Letter)
59. Motorcycle Industry Council
   The New York Times
   Encyclopedia of Associations
60. Motor Vehicle Manufacturers
   Association (MVMA)
61. MVMA
   R.L. Polk & Co. (cited in
   USA Today)
62. *Adweek's Marketing Week*
63. Maritz Marketing Research
64. Maritz Marketing Research
   National Highway Traffic

Safety Administration
   Wellness Letter
65. Maritz Marketing Research
   The Insurance Information
   Institute
66. Gallup
   The New York Times
67. Gallup
68. Gallup
69. Gallup
   USA Today
70. "Single: The New
   Americans" (cited in
   Cosmopolitan)
71. *American Health*
72. Footwear Market Insights
   (cited in *USA Today*)
73. Dr. Scholl's/American
   Podiatry Association
74. Same
75. Same
76. *American Health*
77. *Vanity Fair*
78. *The New York Times*
79. *American Health*
80. *American Health*
81. R.H. Bruskin
82. *Prevention*
83. Clairol
84. Clairol
85. *American Health*
86. Clairol
87. Clairol
88. Clairol
89. Clairol
90. Clairol
91. R.H. Bruskin
92. R.H. Bruskin
93. Gallup
94. Fur Information Council
   The Animals' Agenda
95. *JAMA*
   The Department of the
   Interior
   The Fund for Animals

96. *USA Today*
    Bureau of Justice Statistics
97. *USA Today*
    Bureau of Justice Statistics
    Time
98. *JAMA*
    On An Average Day
99. *American Demographics*
100. The Salvation Army
101. *American Demographics*
102. *American Demographics*
103. *Psychology Today*
     The New York Times
104. Dr. Richard Sipe
105. *The New York Times*
106-7. Bureau of Labor Statistics
     Journal of Occupational
     Medicine
108. *American Demographics*
109. Dr. Scholl's/American
     Podiatry Association
110. General Accounting Office
     USA Today
     Newsweek
110. *Wellness Letter*
     JAMA
112. *Public Health Reports*
113. NORC
     Bureau of Justice Statistics
114. R.H. Bruskin
115. *Psychology Today*
116-17. *The New York Times*
     USA Today
     National Coalition to
     Abolish Corporal
     Punishment
118. Bureau of Justice Statistics
119. DuPont Survivor's Club
     American Body Armor and
     Equipment Company
120. NORC
121. Southern Poverty Law Center
122. NAACP Legal Defense Fund
     National Coalition to Abolish
     the Death Penalty

123. Princeton Religion Research
     Center
124. Barna Research Group
125. Religious News Service
126. NORC
     USA Today
127. NORC
128. Princeton Religion Research
     Center
129. Same
130. Gallup
     Utne Reader
131. NORC
132. *American Demographics*
133. National Christmas Tree
     Association
134. The American Jewish
     Committee
135. Same
136. *American Demographics*
137. Dr. John C. Norcross,
     University of Scranton (cited
     in *USA Today*)
138. Pet Food Institute
     Gallup
     Frosty Paws
139. Same
140. Same
141. Pet Food Institute
     Frosty Paws
142. Gallup
143. *The New York Times*
144. Pet Food Institute
     Frosty Paws
145. American Veterinary Medical
     Association
146. Same
147. *Harvard Environmental Law*
     Review
     Office of Technology
     Assessment
     JAMA
148. *Psychology Today*
149. International Communications
     Research

150. NCHS
151. NCHS
     Psychology Today
152. NCHS
153. *American Health*
154. American Dental Association
155. Procter & Gamble
     JAMA
156. U.S. Department of Health
     and Human Services
157. *In Health*
     JAMA
158. United Network for Organ
     Sharing
     American Medical News
159. Society for the Right to
     Die/Concern for Dying
     The New York Times
160. *Transtime*
161. Roper (cited in *USA Today*)
162. Spiegel, Inc.
163. Korbel Champagne Cellars
164. Same
165. *American Demographics*
166. *JAMA*
     USA Today
167. R.H. Bruskin
168. Same
169. *JAMA*
     American Health
170. Krups, North America
171. Environmental Protection
     Agency
172. John O. Butler Company
173. *The New York Times*
174. Same
175. *American Demographics*
176. *American Journal of Public
     Health*
177. Continental Baking Company
     The New York Times

178. Continental Baking Company
179. Glaxo Inc.
180. *American Journal of Public Health*
181. *The New York Times*
182. Archives of Internal Medicine
183. Calorie Control Council
     Newsweek
184. Calorie Control Council
185. Centers for Disease Control
     National Sporting Goods
     Association
186. *Newsweek*
187. NORC
     A.C. Nielsen
188. Impact Resources, Inc. (cited
     in *USA Today*)
189. *Channels*
190. *Channels*
     Adweek's Marketing Week
191. *Channels*
     The Wall Street Journal (cited in
     Research Alert)
192. "Real Life" (NBC)
193. *Adweek's Marketing Week*
194. Survey Sampling, Inc.
     R.H. Bruskin
195. Maritz Marketing Research,
     Inc. (cited in *USA Today*)
196. Radio Advertising Bureau
197. Same
198. Motion Picture Association of
     America (MPAA)
     Media General Inc.
199. MPAA
200. Roper (cited in Research
     Alert)
201. Media General Inc.
202. Same
203. Hollywood Chamber of
     Commerce
204. R.H. Bruskin

Index

About the Author

Thomas N. **Heymann** is the author of *On An Average Day* (United States), and *On An Average Day In the Soviet Union*, both published by Fawcett Books. In addition to his work as a "people's demographer," Tom Heymann is a marketing consultant and a producer of educational media. He holds a Bachelor of Science degree in Radio, Television, and Film from Northwestern University and an MBA in Marketing from Columbia University. He currently resides in Chappaqua, New York, with his wife, Grace; his son, Gabriel; his daughter, Laura; and his Labrador retrievers, Allie and Grizzly.